TAKE CHARGE!

focused and inspirational advice
for career changers

by

Claire Coldwell

Bloomington, IN  Milton Keynes, UK

authorHOUSE®

AuthorHouse™
1663 Liberty Drive, Suite 200
Bloomington, IN 47403
www.authorhouse.com
Phone: 1-800-839-8640

AuthorHouse™ UK Ltd.
500 Avebury Boulevard
Central Milton Keynes, MK9 2BE
www.authorhouse.co.uk
Phone: 08001974150

First published by AuthorHouse 9/7/2006

ISBN: 1-4259-4671-2 (sc)

Printed in the United States of America
Bloomington, Indiana

This book is printed on acid-free paper.

TAKE CHARGE OF YOUR CAREER!

As a career coach, I see hundreds of people who, having twenty or thirty years' work experience under their belt, have either lost their way in terms of career or admit they never actually found it in the first place. Increasingly, I also see young people who have one or two years' work experience and are disillusioned already.

For both those groups, and many others, each with their own individual story, their experience is that work does not provide the satisfaction or fulfilment which they had hoped to achieve.

Years ago, career paths were generally predictable in that if you knew what you wanted to achieve it was fairly clear how to do it. But things have changed and, while expectations of fulfilment in every area of life have raised over recent decades, such expectations don't come with instructions of how to achieve it. So we are left floundering and inadequate, and if that weren't bad enough, our organisations are now telling us that we have to manage our own career.

Career coaching for adults is something that was unheard of when most of us started work. We had our session with a careers adviser while we were still at school and then we launched ourselves, equipped or not, into the workplace. Some of us found our feet sooner or later and began to carve out what we considered to be a career. Others, more enlightened perhaps, knew they were just beginning a series of jobs.

The quest for career satisfaction is not just about a tweak here and there to get back on track. When people facing a career crisis contact me for help, they come with some fairly substantial questions:

'I'm sure that I have more to offer to the experience of work than this - how do I begin to find out?'

'I believe that there could be a couple of options for my future career — how do I decide what's best for me?

'The job search scene has changed since I was last looking - how do I approach it and market myself effectively?'

'My situation means that I have to stay put in this job for a while — how do I make the best of it?

'There's more to life than work - what about the bigger picture?'

Do any of these questions strike a chord? I hear these every day from people who come to me for career coaching. These people are not unsuccessful or unfocused and they are not waiting for life to drop opportunities in their laps without any effort on their part. They're people like you.

You've probably had a good education and, more than likely, plenty of support and encouragement from your parents; maybe you have set challenging goals for yourself in your early career and have achieved them. You have energy, talent, commitment and a desire to contribute something through your work.

We know that, for our generation, we have greater opportunities and flexibility than previous generations. We've taken hold of those opportunities and we're reaping the rewards. We're earning a good salary and experiencing considerable choice about what we do with our earnings.

Over a period of time, though, you may get a nagging feeling that there's got to be more to life, particularly to work aspects of life – that there must be something more. Maybe you float this notion with your partner, who gives you a look that says 'hmmm, mid-life crisis' or 'hmmm, hormones' depending on your gender.

You talk it through over a drink on a Friday night with your closest friend and he, too, looks at you in disbelief. He points out that you've achieved all you aimed for, you're in line for that 'most wanted' promotion. Your kids are well-adjusted, so what more could you want?

And of course, you couldn't possibly bring up the subject with your parents. You're aware they never had the opportunity to get anywhere close to what you have now, and they've supported you through your education and are so proud of you. You couldn't even hint at a growing feeling that there must be more to life.

'So it's up to me then?'

Many people recognise that it's up to them to make the change in driving their career, but they also accept that they need some help in doing it.

If you really want to be less passive about the proportion of your life which you're spending at work, where to go for advice?

What you need is a trusted adviser who you can call on for succinct, informed advice when you need it – a kind of career agony aunt. What you're sure you don't need is a life-changing programme. You need the equivalent of a phone call or e-mail – sound advice which is specific to the issue which you are grappling with right now, and which will provide immediate direction.

I began to write monthly newsletters to address just this need and made them available on my Web site for clients and ex-clients. Soon strangers, logging in to the site, asked to subscribe, too. The feedback I receive tells me that people appreciate regular, focused career advice to challenge their complacency, make them think differently and keep them on track.

So this book is a collection of those newsletters which covers a range of career questions – those questions which I listed earlier.

This book provides direction in a succinct and digestible way. It's written for people with no time or inclination to make big life changes (at least not right now). It's authoritative, enabling and friendly. At the same time, the approach is inspiring and positive. It therefore addresses the big questions of expressing self through work as well as the immediate issues of writing a great CV. It provides enough information to make you think seriously about taking charge of your career and it provides enough direction and practical advice to build confidence in managing your career without having to work through a step-by-step programme.

I'll be sharing my understanding of careers and what does and does not work in the job arena. At the same time I'll be encouraging you to look at the bigger picture of your own life and how these ideas fit. My approach is not a production line, one-size-fits-all kind of thing. It's about helping you shape and define your individual career in the light of what I'll be presenting you with. I'll be encouraging you to consider what you want for the longer term as well as providing you with immediate practical advice to sort out your current concerns. You'll find that, while you're dealing with the detail of your career transition, you'll be addressing some of life's big issues at the same time.

How to use the book

This is written for people who want career reassurance or guidance – fast! So it's structured in a way which addresses those questions I listed right at the beginning. You can fast forward to those chapters for immediate advice and later, when you have time, read the rest. You'll also notice that I've included some quick reference guides which provide background information to the chapters, drilling down to provide more 'technical' detail, as well as examples, on some of the nitty-gritty HR stuff.

While each chapter is self-contained and will give you the answer you are seeking, the whole book builds a handbook for supporting your career which means that you'll be better able to manage it for the long term.

CONTENTS

Section 1 *'I'm sure that I have more to offer to the experience of work than this – how do I begin to find out?'* *1*

The meaning of work *3*

Quick reference 1: a guide for approaching the questions in this book. 7

New year, new career...............................*10*

Mid-life crisis *13*

What's your story? *17*

Taking control..*22*

The right attitude 26

Don't die! 30

Section 2 *'I believe that there could be a couple of options for my future career – how do I decide what's best for me?* *35*

Myths *37*

Making choices *42*

Quick reference 2: SWOT Analysis *47*

Decisions, decisions............................*50*

Quick reference 3: Force Field Analysis *56*

Plans *59*

Portfolio careers 63

Transferable skills................................*67*

Goals...*72*

Section 3 *'The job search scene has changed since I was last looking*
– how do I approach it and market myself effectively?'.........77

The ultimate CV 83

Quick reference 4: An example
of a chronological CV..87

Quick reference 5: An example of a functional CV..*91*

The truth about older jobseekers........................*95*

Testing, testing...*99*

The interview *103*

Be yourself *108*

The internet and job search *113*

Back to basics..*119*

Staying positive *124*

What really counts *128*

Networking...*132*

The first hundred days.....................................*136*

Section 4 *'My situation means that I have to stay put in this job for a*
while – how do I make the best of it?............................*143*

Politics and career *145*

Mistakes...*150*

Seeing with new eyes..*155*

Little things that make a big difference *160*

Limiting ourselves *166*

Follow my leader?...*170*

Back to work *175*

Eight steps to career success *180*

Section 5 *'There's more to life than work – what about the bigger picture?'* *187*

Work-life balance *189*

What's sacred to you? *193*

Take a break! *196*

So, now what? *201*

Bibliography *203*

SECTION 1

'I'm sure that I have more to offer to the experience of work than this – how do I begin to find out?'

THE MEANING OF WORK

'Life asks of every individual a contribution, and it is up to
that individual to discover what it should be'

Viktor Frankl (1905–1997), developer of existential
psychology and logotherapy; Holocaust survivor.

The questions which clients most often bring to me are - 'How can I get people to see what I have to offer at work?' and 'How do I know what's the right job for me?'

Why are these questions important? Why is work important? The stock answer is because we spend a good deal of our life at work, but that's not the whole story - it's not just about investment of time.

What people are seeking (although they don't always recognise it) is work which expresses their true sense of self. Work which embodies that unique bundle of skills, experiences, talents and perspectives which makes each of us an individual. It's important, not only to be doing work to reflect that sense of self, but to have it recognised by others. In that way it's not just an expression of self, but an extension of self.

That's often why people are so disoriented when they're made redundant - it's not just the loss of material security, it's about the feeling that a fundamental way in which they contribute to the world is no longer valued.

I'm often asked if this viewpoint is realistic. It's hard to believe that people undertaking mundane or unpleasant tasks can feel fulfilled, or that they are expressing themselves through their work. But I constantly come across examples of people doing ordinary jobs, who feel fulfilled. I recall a taxi driver in Florida who kept telling me 'I love my cab! I love it so much that my husband has to drive around with me in order to see me!' And indeed there he was, sharing the experience of Penny contributing to the world of work, running his life from a mobile phone in the front seat of a cab.

What Penny loved about her work was a connection with a variety of people and the ability to provide something for them - efficient transport within an area she knew well. She was clear about what she had to offer and she was fulfilled because she was able to do that.

People I see through my work are often not clear about what they have to offer and not sure whether it's valued. Granted, sometimes it's hard to figure those things out when you've had a lifetime's experience of believing a whole bunch of myths about work. For example: 'You can't be both happy and successful in work'; 'No-one genuinely likes successful people'; 'Work is a drag, and the only reason we do it is to fund an enjoyable leisure time'.

Whenever I read about William Morris, founder of the Arts and Crafts Movement, I'm in awe of the way he expressed himself through work. Last week I read him described as 'poet, designer, craftsman and radical socialist' - all those! And all true! But my first thought was 'They've forgotten painter, architect, historian and lay preacher!' This man knew he had gifts and invoked tremendous energy to express them, even when he wasn't sure quite where it would take him or whether he was likely to be successful. 'Work', he said 'is the embodiment of my dreams'.

I believe that it's within each of us to find work which gives expression to our unique gifts. The process takes time, learning, challenge and a preparedness to ditch the myths we've grown up with, but the difference it makes to dragging yourself out of bed for another dreary day at work or leaping out, eager to contribute in a way which doesn't actually feel like work, is tremendous.

So, where to begin?

I'm a great believer in using energy as a guide. In that first conversation which I have with clients, it doesn't take long to see where their energy is going. Consider what energises you. It may be aspects of your work or leisure, or something which you haven't done for years. Observe how you feel when you think about aspects of work and leisure pursuits. Then dig down to think about what about it energises you. Is it connection with people? Using a particular skill? Being able to help others?

Nick Williams, in his excellent book 'Unconditional Success' says, 'we need to be curious about who we can become and what we can achieve, and let our work be the vehicle for the satisfaction of our curiosity.'

So, get curious! Use these questions as a focus:

-    How would I describe myself and what I have to contribute?
-    How far does my current job reflect that?

- What energises me and what drains me of energy?
- What are the work myths which I embrace?
- What do I want to be known for?
- If I knew that I couldn't fail in my work, what is it that I would do?
- What am I afraid of?

A GUIDE FOR APPROACHING THE QUESTIONS IN THIS BOOK.

The problem with books that set questions, just as I have at the end of Chapter 1, is that you don't have to pay much attention to the quality of your answers. This is the great benefit of working with a career coach in person. They don't let you off the hook. But do yourself a favour, if this is striking a chord with you so far, stop now and read this piece.

It occurs to me that it's all very well asking these searching questions at the end of each chapter, but most people don't have a clue how to approach the answer. If they did, they probably wouldn't be in need of this book.

Okay, well here's an example of how I'd approach one of these questions in a career guidance session, just to give you an idea of how you can begin to challenge yourself.

Me: So what is it you enjoy about your current job?

Nigel: I enjoy managing the guys.

Me: What is it about managing the guys?

Nigel: It's about knowing each of them, their strengths and weaknesses and what they're capable of, and allocating the work according to that. Then they're pleased because the work I allocate them is the right work to get them to achieve the best and quickest results. They're happy, I'm happy and the clients are happy.

Me: So the results are important, too?

Nigel: Yes, I've got to feel that I'm working towards something
        tangible, where I can see the difference I've made with my
        input and know that it's the way that I approached it which
        has made the difference.

Me: So it's not just the results, it's your contribution?

Nigel: I suppose that I've realised that what I really enjoy is being
        at the heart of something successful and knowing that it
        wouldn't have been so successful without me.

Me: Is it just about knowing inside yourself that you make a
        difference or do you need that recognised in some way?

Nigel: Definitely I need that recognised. That's one of the problems
        with the job, that I know that my contribution is really
        important to the success of our unit, but I don't see that it's
        valued by the guys. I think they think that what I do is easy
        and they take it for granted.

Me: So if you had that recognition, how different would your
        job feel?

Nigel: Mmmm, actually, not that different. Yes, it would be nice
        – better than it is now – but I'd still feel a sense of 'Why
        am I here?' It all feels so unimportant.

Me: What's unimportant - what you're contributing?

Nigel: No, not in itself. It's the results. It's what we're there for. In the whole scheme of things I feel that it doesn't matter, we're not contributing anything useful to the world.

Me: So it's the context. You're happy about using your skills but you feel that you could be doing something more useful with them.

Nigel: Yes. I like what I do in that I enjoy the buzz of the office and the challenge of what I do, the personal challenge to me, but at the end of the day what I've achieved doesn't really matter.

Me: So if you could find a job where you are at the heart of things, organising people through understanding their capabilities, juggling priorities and keeping things running, and then that is valued, how would that feel?

Nigel: That would be a great start!

NEW YEAR, NEW CAREER

'Find a way you can contribute to the world - one that utilises your best talents. Build your life around doing what you love to do. Live your life as if it mattered every day that you are alive. This is the way of the heart-centred entrepreneur.'

Sami Sunchild, artist, social innovator, veteran flower child

---

The Christmas and New Year period is often a time which acts as a catalyst for change - a time when one reappraises one's life and, in particular, one's career. All too often, though, a review is brought about by a specific event, either positive, such as good feedback from a key customer or contact (which might make you reconsider your worth outside your current role or organisation), or negative, such as a row with the boss. Focusing on specific events inevitably skews your perception of the true picture.

This skew can be exacerbated, of course, by the alcoholic haze of the seasonal office party which, coincidentally, combines with the opportunity to pour your heart out to an apparently good listener who seems to really understand you - the first time all year that you've felt understood (amazing what a couple of glasses of Bailey's can do, isn't it?). In this enchanted environment, relating your positive experience to an attentive audience leads you to believe that you should be nominated for a service to industry award, at the very least, and relating the negative feedback confirms your suspicions about conspiracy theory and the existence of a Mafiosi element within the organisation.

Believe me, this is not the best environment for making life-changing decisions.

Review your career, by all means, but do it soberly and systematically. Set aside some time for personal review instead of battling it out with other indigestion-ridden folks at the Boxing Day sales. Do a minimum of three hours, get together some facts and look at the whole picture, not just the current job. Make notes on the following:

- Critically evaluate the successes and disappointments of the last year.
- Consider what you have learned about yourself from these.
- How are the above confirmed by feedback from others? If you're not sure, then ask - your boss, clients and colleagues.
- Re-evaluate the market within which you're working - what's likely to happen this coming year?
- How do your skills match up to that?
- How does all of the above fit in to the career plan which you have? Do you need to revise it?
- Do you actually have a career plan?
- Is the work-life balance right for you or do you need to make adjustments? Is anything likely to change this year to affect the balance?

If you structure your thinking around these issues, you are likely to make a more informed decision. Often, a review will tell you that you're in the right job. However, that doesn't mean that it's a waste of time, because it can also provide an indication of what training you might need, which relationships you need to develop and which long-term factors you ought to include in your career plan. Thinking and acting on these has to be good for your organisation, as well as for you. If your review indicates that you're ready for a change, take action now, don't wait another year. If you're confused, seek advice from a career professional.

It is good practice to build in time, regularly, for considering your career and ensuring that you are on track. That way, you ensure that it's part of a wider plan and not just driven by the fact that a new year is looming.

MID-LIFE CRISIS

'Life must be lived forwards but can only be understood backwards'

Kiekergaard Sören, (1813-1855), religious philosopher,
founder of existential philosophy.

Many of my clients are in their early 40s and questioning their career choice - a choice which they made many years ago. Questioning can be putting it mildly - sometimes they're agonising over the fact that it appears that what they've worked for all these years is now meaningless. Sure, they're successful - they've achieved all they set out to at age 18, but the success feels hollow and they are left questioning - 'Is this it?'

My belief is that the issue is about values - that when they set their goals, their values were different. Over the years, with broader and deeper life experiences - which are likely to include marriage, children, bereavement, divorce, illness, redundancy, spiritual awakening, personal achievement - inevitably those values get adjusted.

But often, people are not aware of that adjustment and then the problem is that goals, particularly career goals, don't similarly get adjusted. Questioning those goals, set so long ago, feels somehow as though they are selling out. Partly because when they were set it was a big act of commitment - to self and probably to parents. And to turn away from those goals feels as though you're rejecting something fundamental about yourself and where you've come from.

So, they keep working towards those goals, and the gap between their values and their achievements keeps widening and suddenly, in mid-life they are confronted with the mismatch between the two - often when they've achieved the ultimate goal. It feels all wrong - why?

Some people, confused as to why they feel so unsettled and unhappy, seek to bridge the gap by recreating attitudes and behaviour which they had when their values were different - adopting elements of a previous lifestyle, perhaps - turning on, tuning in and dropping out. They soon discover that this is not the solution: what happens is that it accentuates the gap.

Women, I have observed, are more likely to make an effective adjustment between past and present values on an ongoing basis. They are more often confronted with the mismatch and forced to make choices about it as they go through life. For example, when children come along many women review their values and decide to work part-time, or take a job with less responsibility and greater flexibility. Often not easy decisions to make, granted, but they work through it. So by the time they come to mid life, they might have made three or four adjustments and are relatively comfortable that their work fits their current values set.

Men are more likely to experience the change in values without making a corresponding change in behaviour or goals. (And increasingly I'm seeing this with women who have their first child later in life.) So they can go on for a much longer period of time without having to make a decision. Then when they are confronted with it, the gap seems huge.

How can we deal with all this?

What will solve the issue is reframing the context - spending some time taking a long hard look at your values and how they've changed, accepting it as a natural part of human development and understanding what that means for future goals. It's okay to change your mind - and your goals!

Values change and people change and many of the career crises which I see could be averted by people getting into the habit of periodic reviews of life and career. That way you're focused on what you want to achieve and whether it fits with your sense of self, and you can see if you need to acquire new experiences in order to attain those achievements. Most of all, the process of review enables you to feel comfortable with how your values fit your goals.

So, take stock of where you are right now:

- Take time for regular reviews of your career - at a minimum every six months
- Think about what your current values actually are.
- Consider how your career and life choices reflect your values, and if there's a mismatch, how you can address that. It helps to talk to someone to challenge and support your thinking.

- Use your CV as a focus - it's easier to see the whole picture in black and white. Is that you on paper or does it feel like a stranger?
- Think about the broader picture - what motivates you and energises you? Is that reflected in your CV?
- What does all this mean for the next six months? Do you need to adjust your goals? Do you need training or new development experiences to take you to those goals?
- Encourage your kids to do this - it's a lot easier to build the habit of review when you're young!

WHAT'S YOUR STORY?

A good story cannot be devised; it has to be distilled.

Raymond Chandler (1888-1959), author

and screenplay writer

My great-niece Bethany, not quite three years old, is a bit of a livewire. She has oodles of energy and, even though she's just a little scrap of a thing, keeps the whole family in order. She also loves shopping with the grown-up girlies, but even she started flagging four hours into our Christmas shopping expedition.

So, Great-Aunt Claire took the opportunity to find a free square-foot of carpet in M&S and I sat on the floor reading to her while the rest of the family carried on shopping. We had a blissful half-hour, interrupted only by passing toddlers who joined us briefly before being moved on, rather reluctantly, I thought, by their parents.

Bethany and I can get absorbed in stories to the exclusion of everything else and we emerge from the depths of a book with new energy. What is it about stories that energises us? Is it just 'time out'? I think it's the ability to take us to another world, to give us a different perspective, to make us see that there's more outside our own lives. That sounds grandiose - Bethany just enjoyed being entertained, of course, but the world of The Little Mermaid, a world of underwater princesses and earth princes, of magic and trickery and true love winning the day was just about as far removed from a shopping mall in December as you can get and that was okay with me, too.

Christmas is a time when old familiar stories, either on the page or on screen, get a re-run. It's also a time for catching up on the 'stories' of friends and family, sometimes in person but more often in an eight-word summary on a Christmas card. Stories are important in making sense of our world and we often come across imagery about stories when we are discussing our life and career. We speak of 'new chapters' or a 'new page' when we are looking for (or thrust into) a new direction. We can see our life as a story, and often when I'm meeting a new client I'll start off by saying 'What's your story?', which is shorthand for saying 'What are the events which led you to believe that you need some career coaching at this point in your life?' Many people get stuck because they haven't figured out the next chapter; they can't see the next step and they need someone to help them to find the options.

I'm just reading a great book called What Should I Do With My Life – see bibliography for details – and the author begins thus: 'We are all writing the story of our life. We want to know what it's 'about', what are its themes and which theme is on the rise…we want to know where we're headed – not to spoil our own ending by ruining the surprise, but we want to ensure that when the ending comes, it won't be shallow. We will have done something. We will not have squandered our time here. This book is about that urge, that need.'

He's right. We want to make some sort of sense of it all. People often come to me because they can't make sense of the story-so-far and haven't got a clue what that means for the story-to-come. It seems as though this is all there is and they can't seem to envisage how the next chapter might move things on.

Sometimes using the idea of a story in a very direct way can help you to find your next move. I recall a powerful exercise I did earlier this year (I think it came from Julia Cameron's excellent book, The Artist's Way) where I wrote a letter from me at age 80 to me now. I approached the exercise with some excitement – what would I discover? In the letter, I talked about the way in which my life had unfolded and the key events which had taken place, and I found that I was telling myself that the things which were concerning me in 2004 turned out to have no importance at all, in the whole scheme of things. I gave myself some advice about what to focus on and to watch out for (though I did point out to myself that I'm not good at taking advice from anyone, and undoubtedly that includes an older and wiser me). The benefit of that kind of exercise is that not only does it help you to see that there is more than one way forward, but it shifts you out of inertia. Life, after all, does move on, whether you take a passive or an active role, so you may as well shape it for yourself.

I often advise clients to talk to other people who may be doing the work which they might like to do or might have come from a similar background. The benefit of that is not to consider it to be a template for the only, or even the best, way to do things – it's to encourage people to 'try it on for size'. It's about weighing it up and seeing if that's a likely move. To put yourself in their shoes and to think 'How would I feel about that?'

Some of my favourite stories have more than one ending. Did you ever see Sliding Doors? I love the thought that life could be like that - you could nudge it this way or another, slightly different, move could nudge it that way. But there are options for all of us – there's more than one way a story could evolve. How different would that be!

Think about what you're putting up with and accepting as a given - just tolerating - and consider if that is truly a block to a better future or just a perceived block. Either way, if you were writing your life as a story, you'd make the central character do something about it – well, wouldn't you! Otherwise, how is the story going to move on?

Often when we're stuck there has to be an intervention to shift things significantly. For the Little Mermaid, she needed legs. Her fishtail, gorgeous though it was, was going to be no use to her in achieving her heart's desire. If you've always had a tail and you realise you now need legs, that is not an easy thing either to accept or to achieve. The Little Mermaid needed intervention in the form of magic and she had to make sacrifices. She had to risk loss – certainly loss of her fishtail and a familiar lifestyle, but also potentially the love of her father and her beautiful voice. Clearly, she thought it was worth it – the potential gains outweighed the likely losses. Telling your story helps you to consider what interventions are needed and again, how you might feel about those.

So when you're updating family and friends with the events of the past year, keep a piece of your mind focused on the story you're telling. Consider which are the key elements that come to the surface and which are the bits that you're not recounting. What does that tell you? The benefit of telling your story to others is that they are likely to spot things which you haven't noticed. Listen to their views and consider their responses.

Then, most importantly, take a little time out to think about next year's update. Write it down! So you'll begin 'You recall that last year I'd told you that…..Well, what happened next was…..' Provide a few options, try them on for size and see what you feel about them. You may well want to pursue them in reality.

TAKING CONTROL

'One that would have the fruit must climb the tree'

Thomas Fuller (1608-1661), physician, preacher and scholar.

Poor old Sven-Goran Eriksson. Again discovered having secret meetings under cover of darkness. This time not to do with matters of the heart (or other parts of the anatomy) but to do with a potential next job.

Nevertheless, was the British public any more tolerant? Not a bit of it! Now, I'm not at all interested in football so maybe you'll think I'm naïve, but I was amazed by the outrage that ensued. For several days the TV news (even local news) would give at least a few minutes' airtime to allow Joe Public to express his views on Sven's behaviour. It seems that the disloyalty and disrespect which people had felt that Sven had demonstrated in his relationship with Nancy totally and completely paled into insignificance when it was discovered that he was exploring options for a new job.

Poor old Sven-Goran. He was then forced into making a statement of intention. To put all his cards on the table and tell the world exactly where his loyalty lay - both now and for the future. I really don't recall such fervour about his loyalty for Nancy.

Anyway, perhaps I am naïve but I was surprised at the reaction. Don't people keep their antennae out for job opportunities all the time? As a career management practitioner, this is what I advise clients to do. No harm in looking.

I think some of the excitement was that football fans honestly did feel that Sven-Goran was being disloyal by seeking opportunities elsewhere. Perhaps (as was all too clearly demonstrated in his liaison with Ulrika) people weren't convinced that he was simply and solely 'window shopping' and that some action was bound to result. But it doesn't make sense to apply the same implicit or explicit groundrules for jobs as you might for personal relationships.

I spend a good deal of my time talking to clients about the shift in the psychological contract with employers. The expectation of jobs for life which our parents might have experienced has long since gone. We now embark upon work relationships with both employer and employee understanding that there won't be a job until retirement.

But this doesn't mean that the relationship is any less sound. The expectations are that individuals will move on much more rapidly to other companies, that companies expect employees to provide a high level of skills and expertise for a shorter period of time and in return they will be paid a high salary with good benefits plus the opportunity to develop their expertise, which is understood will transfer to new situations at some point. It's a short-term investment.

But short-term doesn't mean second-best. Both parties win. They both get what they need. The trick for employers is to try to keep the employee motivated for as long as they have the expertise which is required by the company. That way they'll stay. The trick for the employee is to try to ensure that they remain adequately rewarded for the time they stay and that they remain employable so that they are able to move on to the right position at the right time.

When both those align, that's great. It seems that Sven-Goran and his current employer managed to reach an understanding about what I've outlined above, at least for now.

But we can't expect that it will be great forever. Companies change in order to remain competitive and along with that change comes requirements for new skills and new structures. So that can mean that individuals who were once valued are no longer crucial to the future of the business. From the individual's point of view, they change too, and often want to use their particular skills in a way which they recognise is just not going to happen in their current company, for a whole variety of reasons. So inevitably there comes a time when the two parties have less need for each other than was the case at the outset.

What career management practitioners aim to do is to encourage our clients to recognise when the optimum time to move on might be. In order to do this you need to be aware of two key things: what you have to offer and what the market has to offer.

Ways to achieve the former are through being open to feedback, by understanding where your strengths and weaknesses are, by being clear about your values and skills. Ways to achieve the latter are by understanding how your industry is developing and how your own development reflects that.

Once you are clear about all these, then you need conversations to make sure that key people who might provide opportunities are aware of the type of role you are looking for. These conversations might provide immediate openings but, more likely, they'll provide a foundation which will be built on by further conversations over a period of time and result in opportunities later on.

This is what Sven-Goran was doing. It's good career management because, really, you don't want to wait until a move is necessary before you start these conversations. The chances of getting closer to what you want are higher if you start ahead of need. You can shape the role and negotiate the best deal. That way the control is at least equal between you and your prospective employer, if not balanced in your favour. And control over your future is really what you're aiming for.

Maybe Sven-Goran's sin, on reflection, was not that he was exploring options, but that he was caught looking. Nobody likes their plans to be made public before they're ready. Ah well, I guess that's the price of fame.

So:

- Understand your skills and what you have to offer
- Keep tuned in to how your chosen job market is developing.
- Maintain your skills base in line with this – that means taking opportunities for new experiences within your current role as well as taking opportunities for training.
- Maintain a network of key contacts who understand, at any time, you, your skills and potential.

THE RIGHT ATTITUDE

'If you think you can, you can. And if you think you can't,

you're right'

Mary Kay Ash (1915 -), entrepreneur

My friends would tell you that I don't watch much TV. I can usually find some other form of entertainment more appealing, but now and then something on the box captures my imagination. So it is with the series 'Faking It', where individuals have four weeks to learn how to do a totally different job so competently that even the experts can't tell that they haven't been doing it all their life. I find it fascinating.

The last programme of the last series was about a chorister - a classically-trained singer and a Christian, who was due to fake a performance as a rock singer.

Her mentors, a couple of sassy chicks from the rock world, spent every waking hour preparing her for this performance in terms of developing her singing style, overhauling her wardrobe and make-up, taking her to rock venues to soak up the ambience and generally get immersed in the lifestyle, but with limited success. The day before the final performance they had to conclude that it wasn't convincing. The problem? 'She's up for it, but she needs to change her attitude'.

We learn about the importance of attitude from an early age when it can pop up with alarming regularity on school reports - 'Jimmy has the ability to be top of the class but his attitude lets him down'. A positive and focused attitude is important in approaching new goals because behind it lies energy and motivation, so we know that when the attitude is appropriate then we are likely to make a success of what we are doing.

If you're not up for something then it shows, even if you talk a good talk, and that has been apparent with hundreds of the people I've interviewed during the years I spent recruiting. Many people who are suitably qualified and with the right experience don't cut it, yet many people who are lacking in relevant experience secure the job they're after because they have the right attitude - they are energised and enthusiastic and often better informed, too. A recent Harvard study found that 20% of success is due to credentials and 80% to self-belief.

On that basis, I often tell people to approach an interview as though they have the job already. Sounds a bit odd, doesn't it, but it's not about being pushy. It's about thinking yourself into the mindset of being in the job so that when you answer questions it's from a different perspective. I applied this approach myself very recently when I was being considered for a role which I really wanted. I was nervous before the meeting, not sure if this role was really a step too far, but then I thought of my advice to clients and how I'd better apply it to myself. It worked! I was given the role and, as a bonus, the whole meeting felt comfortable and energised.

But as the school reports indicate, it's hard to demonstrate a positive attitude if you don't have the heart for it, and this is often the case when we're working on someone else's goals. Why don't we always have the energy for it when we've set our own goals, though?

Part of the problem for the chorister in adopting a rock chick persona was that her attitude was all tied up with her values, which were strongly held. So she was never going to truly get under the skin of some of the behaviours if she felt that she was selling her soul in order to do it - many aspects of the changes required were, for her, challenging her principles. She had made personal commitments on which she was not prepared to compromise, and even though it was her decision to 'fake it', when she was asked to demonstrate behaviours which suggested principles she didn't hold, she just couldn't do it.

When I work with new clients we often spend some time exploring values. This is important because if you have the right skills and experience for a job and your values don't align with the company you are approaching, then the fit isn't going to be there, and try as you might to change, it won't really work. The best you'd achieve would be a change in superficial behaviour but a knowledge that what you are underneath is entirely different. I wouldn't recommend living that kind of double life for long. It's too draining for anything other than a short-term job assignment.

It is possible, of course, to change your attitude by 'reframing' the way in which you perceive things - we don't have to repeat negative past experiences.

Other tips to develop a positive attitude are:

- Think longer term, beyond the challenges of the current situation to the rewards which lie ahead
- Be clear about what you have to offer and remind yourself of them frequently - keep a list to hand
- Seek positive feedback from others as to your best qualities
- Surround yourself with positive and supportive people
- Understand your values and why you want the change/job/opportunity - what really motivates you?
- If this is not a goal you set yourself ask yourself if you really want it enough to go for it
- Get the right perspective. Remind yourself that this job/change/opportunity is only one aspect of your life. Take time for energising experiences in other areas of your life.

DON'T DIE!

A fellow career practitioner was telling me about the oldest client he'd worked with. The client, Morris, was 89 and had just been made redundant, so was seeking career advice to support him in finding his next opportunity.

STOP!!!

Just stop there for a second and understand that. Eighty-nine years old. He could well have rolled over and thought 'Fair enough, I reckon I've given all that I have to give; time to call it a day'. But no! His approach was 'What's next!'

This up-for-it attitude was illustrated at a birthday party that my friend Mark, and his team, gave when Morris reached 90. One of the youngsters in the office asked him the classic birthday question 'To what do you attribute your great age?' Morris's response was 'Don't die!'

This apparently flummoxed the youngsters, who were expecting some sage and profound recipe for longevity, but how complicated do you have to make it? You wanna live long? Then don't die!

There's more.

It turns out that Morris had been born deaf and only began to hear at the age of 60, when his wife came across a cure for his particular form of deafness, so it was into his seventh decade that he gained a new lease of life, now able to contribute in a different way – giving and receiving to others, and not just to the national economy.

This (true) story has a few messages for me – and therefore for you. Morris was clearly someone who was not going to passively accept his lot as being boxed up in any particular way which might limit his contribution. Old? Disabled? Maybe so, but not disadvantaged. His approach meant that, rather than viewing life in terms of limitations, instead he was looking for particular types of opportunities which fitted with his capabilities and aspirations.

I see many people who respond to my suggestions for progress with 'Yes, but I can't/ I couldn't/ I've never…..' They have a list of objections and reasons why not before I've even finished formulating my sentence. I never met Morris but I imagine his responses would be more along the lines of 'Let's look how I could achieve that, given that…' 'Could I do it this way?'…'I've been thinking of this – could it work?....' This approach puts you in a different place altogether.

The message here is that Morris was looking at himself and his unique qualities rather than in stereotypical terms. How often do we look at ourselves in terms of categories – redundee; 50 year-old; unskilled – rather than concentrating on our individuality and what we have to offer. We do need to manage the way in which others' view us, so if we concentrate on what we see as limiting factors in ourselves, then others will, too.

You only have to look around at some great examples of older people – Twiggy, in her 50s, modelling long after the usual sell-by date for those in her profession; Joan Bakewell in her 70s, an intellect as sharp as ever it was and still a force to be reckoned with – and to hear of countless examples of people not limited by physical or other constraints, to realise that boundaries and limitations are often self-imposed. Who says you can't do it? Don't die!

We've all heard of the self-fulfilling prophecy, where the evidence is that things frequently turn out just as we expect, not because we're psychic, but because we behave in a manner which optimises those very outcomes. We create the circumstances where those things will come to pass – and guess what? They do. So it could be a good idea to accentuate the positive, huh?

Sometimes this is hard when we feel war-weary in terms of career. How we have to draw upon our energy to talk about our career history – 'Must I? Again?' But here's a tip to energise you:

I was at a networking Masterclass last week where the speaker encouraged us to introduce ourselves giving personal and distinctive information. This is far more memorable, he suggests, than focusing on all that business stuff. Not only is it more memorable but it also puts you much more in control. You may eventually get to the bits about you which aren't so riveting, but you can pitch it so that the things you are proud of and which are more distinctive or simply more fun come first. So....'I once played in a rock band – with cardboard guitars.....'; ' I once did a parachute jump....' Try it. You'll feel more comfortable and confident and less intense. A good place to be.

I take another message from Morris's story, too, which is about time management. Not in the day-to-day Filofax sense, but managing time over the career span – taking a view of the whole picture, not just discrete blinkered bits. If you're more focused on possibilities and opportunities than limitations and you take a proactive view of your contribution in the workplace it figures that you're not biding your time until retirement. The whole career picture takes a different perspective. Thinking of Morris, I get an image of him seeing life and opportunities stretching out ahead into infinity, rather than seeing a cliff edge after which there's a drop into the void. After all, if you're a Morris, then where does retirement fit into the picture, anyway? And I'm thinking, if you approach life in that way, it has tons more energy injected into it – it's going to keep you bounding along at a fair pace, just as long as you want to go on.

In order to think about what the next appropriate opportunity out there might be, you need two things – one to be aware of your own capabilities, skills and aspirations; and two to be aware of what's out there. This is neither about ignoring your limitations nor about fitting into some pre-defined roles for people like you – grey, unskilled, inexperienced (those categories again). It's about taking a look at you as an individual and matching it up to the opportunities out there. To really get the edge, think ahead to opportunities for emerging businesses, think about what's happening in organisations and what they might need from you.

Think. Research. Act. Get on with it. Don't die!

SECTION 2

'I believe that there could be a couple of options for my future career – how do I decide what's best for me?

MYTHS

There are plenty of myths surrounding Christmas. Such as: Jesus was born on December 25th; Three wise men visited the infant Jesus; Xmas is a disrespectful abbreviation for the word Christmas; Santa was invented by Coca Cola.

Those are some myths, now here are the facts. No-one knows when Jesus was born; 'Three Wise Men' was probably a reference to three stars which were in the sky at the time of Jesus' birth; The X in Xmas represents the Greek letter Chi, the first letter of Christos, meaning Christ; The original Santa Claus originated from Turkey - he was a generous bishop who gave to the poor, once leaving some gold in a stocking which had been hung out to dry.

What's all this to do with careers?

Well there are facts and there are myths and often we lose distinction between the two. And that applies to careers as much as it does to Christmas.

Where do myths come from? Who knows? Sharing stories about what's important in life helps us to form an idea of reality and what we're dealing with. They can be a way of explaining the unexplainable and of providing parallel experiences so that we can illustrate concepts, ideas and moral issues so that we can learn how to go about life. They help us to make sense of the world around us and how we fit into it. In providing an understanding based on others' experiences they can predict what we will be dealing with and that predictability can shape our behaviour.

Now this is where it starts to get dodgy, especially when the perpetuated wisdom is somewhat removed from the original fact. Stories get distorted as they are handed down through the generations and they then assume a life of their own. So if we're basing our behaviour on something that's a myth rather than reality we have the potential, at worst, to make a serious mistake or at best, we're likely to miss out on something.

So if you really believe that Santa Claus drops down the chimney with a bundle of goodies on Christmas Eve then you may well be disappointed before December is out (unless you have some very obliging friends and family in which case the myth has shaped their behaviour as well as yours).

What are some of the myths surrounding careers? Here are a few. 'It's easier to get a job when you're in a job'; 'A decision about appointment is made in the first 30 seconds of an interview'; 'If I put my age on my

CV it'll automatically get assigned to the reject pile'; 'It's harder to get a look in if you've been made redundant'.

These notions are unsubstantiated by research, though you may hear many people talking as though they are reality. And of course they might be reality for a few people in a few situations, but you have to cut through all this to understand that these are not Universal Truths.

And of course whether you believe that they are truths or not is neither here nor there unless they affect your behaviour. The problem is that they do affect behaviour. So what I see a lot of is that people don't take action because they think that the result is a foregone conclusion - they're too old, too young, not qualified enough, over qualified, the wrong sex... the list goes on. So then the belief is that there's no point in even applying for work because they'll fall at the first hurdle. And I hear so many times the above given as justification for not applying for jobs.

How realistic is this? I know that I'm often accused of being perpetually optimistic but I'm not suggesting that you ignore the facts. I'd just ask you to think about how helpful it might be to you to perpetuate these myths for yourself. It's not at all helpful if it's going to prevent you moving on.

How do such myths make us feel? Helpless? Inadequate? Out of control, perhaps? You don't need to feel like this. Create your own reality. Weigh up for yourself what the experience is. Don't decide that something is reality before you've checked it out. That means taking action. If you apply for a job and they tell you you're not qualified enough, then that is probably the reality for that particular situation. But you don't know that before you've applied and it's not going to be the case for every application. That approach is called looking for problems.

Now here's a fact. FACT, I said. I know someone who, during her working life, has been appointed, not once, but five times, to a job for which she was not qualified. How? Because she was convinced that she could do it, that's how. And being convinced, she managed to convince the people she needed to influence.

I also know of someone who it was suggested was too old and didn't have the 'right experience' to get a new idea off the ground and change career. So, undaunted by this and with the courage of his convictions he set up his own business to turn his idea into reality, successfully.

Every day I hear of people who've pushed aside the myths of jobsearch to find a new opportunity.

Explode the myths:

- Don't talk yourself out of a job change at the starting block but do your research. Move from an area of unknown to an area which is known. Know yourself and know your opportunity. If you've done your homework then there's no reason why you shouldn't get the opportunities you are seeking.
- Consider each situation as a new one, so don't get daunted by the 'I've tried that before and it didn't work' syndrome. This is a new situation, you've done your homework, you're not depending on luck but sound research, so on that basis it's worth a try.
- Get feedback. So if you're not selected this time find out why and then use that information to shape your ongoing jobsearch.

- I know I often say this, but here it is again. Steer clear of those who are pessimistic and try to talk you out of your plan. Go with your belief and your research. You know best.
- Use the opportunity for learning. What do you discover about yourself? Do you get any more clarity on what you really want?

MAKING CHOICES

'Those who say no can also say yes'

Anon

What a great quotation that is. A truism. Fundamental in its truthfulness and its simplicity.

Or, another way of putting it, blindingly obvious.

But don't we lose sight of this simplicity so often? We tie ourselves up in knots when we are confronted with a choice. We so often tell ourselves that we don't have any choice - that someone else is holding all the cards, making the decisions for us - our hands are tied. Or if we think we do have a choice, we agonise over making the 'right' choice, whatever that is.

Does it have to be that complicated, even for major life decisions?

Even if we don't have a great deal of choice about our current situation, for example for those of my clients in a redundancy situation, you can choose how to respond. Do you lie down and play dead or do you use it as a wake-up call to a new future - one which you hadn't previously envisaged?

Choice, at its most fundamental, is simple, not complex. There are, essentially, only two ways we can react - to accept what we have or to move on to something. Surrender or shift. The key is not to do either without conviction, and the way to make a decision from a place of conviction is to be truly grounded. If you are not grounded, you stay put out of fear and rigidity or you move on too often - you have no staying power. When you are grounded you are clear about what you need to do and your action is from a place of strength.

Being grounded gives you structure, stability and security.

Oh, so that's easy then......

Those of you who have experienced redundancy or have been a victim of restructuring at work might have read the sentence before last and wondered what planet I'm on. Structure, stability and security - where, pray? Haven't had a sniff of any of those for a while. Wasn't that the 80s boom?

You're right to be sceptical. Those things can't be relied upon on out there. The only structure, stability and security you can depend upon is what's inside you - your own resourcefulness.

How do you get a grip on your own resourcefulness? Two ways, I'd say.

The first way - from knowing yourself - how you really are, not how you think you are, what you have to offer, and what your personal values are.

Self-awareness is the key here. For if you know what are your strengths and shortcomings then you're well placed to deal with the situation - any situation - you can learn to use your strengths to counteract your weaknesses. So, personality profiling (completing a questionnaire to tap into your individual style and preferences for the way in which you go about things) can be useful here, otherwise any feedback is useful.

Other ways to understand yourself are to accept and understand conflicting emotions. Differentiate between what arises from a feeling that you 'should' do something and that which feels more true to your nature.

Evaluate your past experiences - how you've made choices in the past - have you fallen into jobs or made a proactive choice? Be wary of repeating past choices automatically. Think through how it worked (or didn't) for you last time. Wanna do it differently this time? You could, you know.

The second way - there is also strength to be gained from knowledge about the external environment - the opportunities available, and how they relate to you.

Find out what's out there. It takes investment in time and energy. It might challenge your preconceptions. It might even blow your mind. Be prepared for that. But do it. One thing is for sure - you'll learn something, even if it's that you'd rather stay put for now.

Don't flounder in indecision. Get together a strategy for deciding, that'll make you feel more in control. It may be a SWOT analysis or force-field analysis. Identify the decision-making strategies that work for you.

One of my personal favourites is a SWOT analysis. In picking apart the strengths, weaknesses, opportunities and threats of a situation (and there is usually something which you can put under each heading) you make the whole thing more manageable and begin to understand what you're dealing with. When you do that exercise, you may not have all the information you need right then, but it does provide a way of highlighting exactly what you do need to find out, so again, can shift you out of inactivity.

I'm one of life's great list-makers. I recall that when I was confronted with the biggest decision of my life, my strategy was to compile a list, or rather, two lists – reasons to stay and reasons to move on. After four hours and careful thought, I had twenty-two items in the 'reasons to stay' column and when I turned to the 'reasons to go' could come up with only one. But seeing it there in black-and-white I knew the course of action which was right for me – to move on. No doubt about it. Sometimes getting it down on paper is what it needs; sometimes it's talking it over with someone. Whatever works for you, do it.

By the way, you might have gathered by now that a theme is emerging. This, ALL this, can be summed up in two words – taking responsibility. Choice means responsibility.

You often hear about people who faced and worked through a crisis who go on to make unprecedented changes in other aspects of their life. I'm sure that it's not because they get hooked on change and crisis – it's because they suddenly realise with crystal clarity what depths of resources they have at their disposal. Take those steps to understand what you're dealing with – you'll never look back.

And isn't this grappling with choice just such an essential part of being human? Embrace it. Relish it - it's always going to be there!

- Set aside some time to make decisions – don't think that they will make themselves while you go about your everyday life.
- Understand yourself – skills, experiences, emotions, personality, values, and make your decisions against that backdrop. Ignoring factors which are a crucial part of you won't work.
- Find a decision-making strategy which works for you.
- Do the groundwork. Even if it doesn't resolve itself there and then, you'll have shifted something in your mind and prepared the way for a decision.

SWOT ANALYSIS

SWOT analysis is a tool for evaluating situations and is especially useful in making comparisons between two choices. So, in career move terms, it helps to weigh up the various merits of different options, which may be similar, such as the choice between two different jobs, or may be quite different, such as, for example, the choice between a job offer and a retraining option.

SWOT stands for **strengths, weaknesses, opportunities, and threats.** Strengths and weaknesses tend to be **internal** factors. Opportunities and threats tend to be **external** factors.

Strengths	Weaknesses
Opportunities	Threats

For example:

A **strength** could be:

- your specialist expertise in your professional field/sector.
- your experience with a particular product
- business experience, eg supporting a merger, international working
- flexibility (to relocate etc)
- particular qualifications

A **weakness** could be:

- lack of a particular expertise
- lack of flexibility
- lack of experience
- lack of required qualifications
- unattractive terms of employment

An **opportunity** could be:

- a move to a developing market.
- moving into a sector which offers scope for promotion
- possibilities for new learning

A **threat** could be:

- a job which might turn out to be 'dead end'
- lack of knowledge about potential opportunities
- a 'buyers market'

- misalignment with your values and those of the recruiting organisation

SWOT analysis can, of course, be very subjective so it should be viewed as a means of prompting your thinking rather than as the definitive picture. What often happens is that the exercise highlights gaps in knowledge so it's useful as a catalyst for finding out more information.

Also, be aware that the option with the greatest number of strengths isn't necessarily the one which you might go for! Often, in committing your thoughts to paper, you are better able to evaluate what's entailed and you may well decide that the opportunities of one option, though limited, might be so outstanding that they far outweigh the many strengths of another.

DECISIONS, DECISIONS

'It doesn't matter which side of the fence you get off on sometimes. What matters most is getting off. You cannot make progress without making decisions.'

Jim Rohn, speaker, philosopher and entrepreneur.

I'm generally someone who is comfortable to make decisions alone – ranging from the choice between paella or chilli con carne for dinner to which house to buy. This month, though, I seem to have been swamped by decisions to make – about which work to focus on and when; decisions about major purchases for my home; decisions about changing the way I run my business; decisions about how exactly I'm going to fit in a new aspect to my life – visits to the gym - with the other things I have to juggle. When you have lots to juggle, you can feel overwhelmed and that's when the doubts set in – 'Am I doing the right thing?' and 'How can I possibly decide?'

Life seems hectic for everyone. I'm sure that somewhere there are published measures on how the pace of life has stepped up in the last century, and we seem to be faced with more options and increased pressure to choose between them. The decisions which we are making always seem to be at the expense of something else - 'If I do this, it means I can't do that'. And yes, we want to do the right thing, make the best decision, whatever that is. Sometimes, even if we're strong decision-makers, it seems impossible to know what's the right thing, and the bigger the decision, the more money and greater number of people implicated or the further ranging the effect, the harder it is to do with confidence.

Decisions about career are never easy (actually, for some people they might seem to be, but I'll come back to that). The difficulty is that we're often looking into the unknown, that is, you might be stepping into unfamiliar territory and the success or otherwise of your choice will not be known immediately.

So, you might be considering a new direction, and you're embarking upon that without knowing one hundred per cent whether it's right for you. What often complicates it further is that you might have to make a prior decision before you make that decision, so for example, retrain before you even begin that career, so the time whether you'll know it was the right decision may be quite some way off, by which time you'll be committed to it and it will be difficult to change.

And of course, decisions are often multi-faceted. So, to continue the example above, it's mostly not just 'Am I prepared to retrain for a new career?' It's more like, 'If I re-train (and we're still at the 'if' stage here, you notice), do I study by distance learning and keep earning, or do I give up work and study full time? And if I keep earning, do I stay where I am, in a job which might not give me the time I need to study or do I find a job which has less responsibility and might be closer in nature to my ultimate career aim?'.

And then… 'and which of those would fit best with my partner and the kids, and does that mean that we'll have to buy a smaller house or change some other aspect of our lifestyle?'.

And maybe even more…. 'and what if my partner gets the promotion she's hoping for in a year's time? If I start the distance learning option, I could have gone for the full time and been halfway to finishing my course, so distance learning wouldn't have been the best option'.

And ultimately….'Then what if, when I've qualified I can't get a job?'

It's no wonder that people stay where they are. Daunted by the unknown, it feels far better to hang on and work slowly towards the pension – the one good thing about the job, even if the fulfilment factor scores only 3 out of 10.

I said that decisions do come easily for some. Yes, there are those who are so convinced of the right course of action that you couldn't deter them from it if you told them that you could see into the future and it wasn't looking at all good. We often envy that clarity, don't we, because they just sweep aside objections and obstacles and find a way to do what they feel they need to do.

I think we can all become more comfortable with making decisions by taking an approach which considers the following elements - values and knowledge.

In terms of values, if we are clear about what we stand for then it's easier to decide our route in life. This is probably at the heart of why people in the category I mentioned above find it easy to make decisions – the change that they believe they need to make is about something which is at the core of what they see themselves standing for. This is often born out of less-than-happy experiences at work or in life where they get to the point that they know for certain that they are not going to tolerate this or that any more. They'll shift out of it, whatever it takes.

Values are at the core of our expectations of life and the clearer we are about our values, the clearer we are about our expectations, so that gives greater certainty to our decision-making.

Conversely, if we are finding that some decisions are extremely difficult to make, then we can often find that at the heart of it is conflicting values. If you've been struggling with a decision, set aside some time to think it through in depth. Are there two or more principles which you're trying to remain true to, but in doing so you've arrived at a stalemate?

Steven Covey's The Seven Habits of Effective People puts values as an important factor in being effective. If you are clear on your values then your decisions become driven by that, from career choice to reviewing your schedule each morning for the day ahead.

For some people, living according to their values is based on gut feel, so they just 'know' what the right course of action is without articulating it. For others, they can express it clearly. Other people might say that they are not at all clear - they might consider that understanding their values is something they don't give much thought to. However, it just takes some self-reflection and observation to figure it out. You may not express beliefs or codes for behaviour but listen to yourself talking and it will become clear what are the principles by which you live your life - what you see as fair or unfair, how you spend your money and your time; what you resent doing and what you put yourself out for.

Once you've really thought about it, as I say, you might be faced with a conflict that you had been ignoring, but this is all food for thought and you won't be able to move ahead without dealing with it.

And then there's knowledge. It sounds self-evident to say that it's difficult to make a decision without knowledge, but many people take that approach. Look at the example I gave above of the individual considering retraining – much of this could be clarified, but people often get so caught up in the burden of decision-making that they don't start to pick their way through. The more that you can shift your thinking from the unknown to the known, the more comfortable you will be with your decision.

One good tool to use is force-field analysis. A force-field analysis is a way of encouraging you to look at the elements in your current situation which are propelling you towards your goal and the elements which are inhibiting you from achieving it. Once you've worked through that you can review ways to minimise the inhibitors and accentuate the propellers. This is often best worked through with someone else so that you can get the benefit of their ideas - chances are if you're feeling stuck that you're blinkered as to how to improve the situation.

It's hard to be objective, so work these exercises through with a friend or your partner – someone else who can be objective and who can challenge you. Don't expect a comfortable experience, though. This is often why people choose to work with a career coach – they know they will get that objective focus which eluded them elsewhere. True, some of this stuff can be very close to home and difficult to talk through with a partner or family member.

So, instead of floundering around wondering why you can't make a decision, set aside some time to confront it head on. Then you can begin to move on.

FORCE FIELD ANALYSIS

Force field analysis is a diagnostic technique developed by Kurt Lewin, a pioneer in the field of social sciences. It is a technique which is useful when looking at the factors impacting upon change and particularly in identifying the blocks to progression.

Lewin's model suggests that in any situation there are both driving and restraining forces.

DRIVING FORCES

Driving forces are those forces affecting a situation which are pushing in a particular direction; they tend to initiate a change and keep it going. In terms of career change, examples might be desire for change, drive for improvement, self-belief, support from others, etc

RESTRAINING FORCES

Restraining forces are forces acting to restrain or decrease the driving forces. Examples might be fear of failure, lack of specific skills skills or experience, loss of status etc. The theory goes that equilibrium is reached when the sum of the driving forces equals the sum of the restraining forces but equilibrium in the career change context can mean inertia!

So what we're aiming to do is to shift you from that inertia state into one of action. How do we do that?

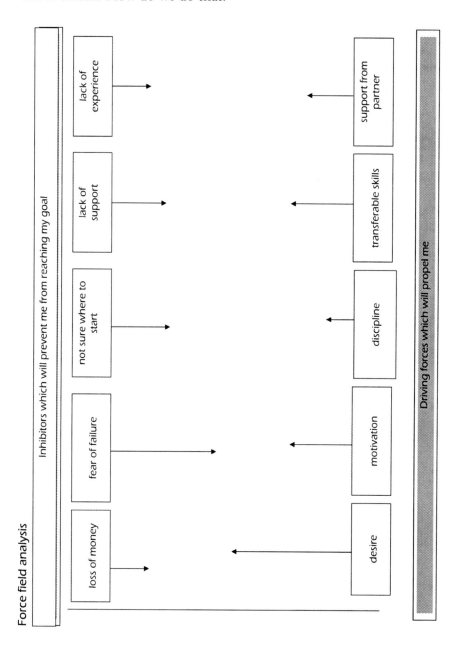

Force field analysis

The first thing to do is to evaluate the restraining forces. To what extent are they perceived or real barriers? Some, as in the example above, will be tangible and some less so, and you may need someone to challenge you to get an objective perspective.

Then consider how you can boost the driving forces and diminish the effects of the restraining ones. Put an action plan in place to address these.

When I'm working on this with a client I always think of a hot air balloon, all puffed up and ready to go, straining at the ropes which keep it grounded. The task is to cut those ropes, one by ones, to set you free!

PLANS

'Life is what happens to you while you're busy making other plans'

John Lennon (1940-1980), singer and songwriter

I love that quote. I often use it to illustrate how some people can rumble on in a job for years, thinking that at some stage they'll make a decision about where they really want to be and seriously begin to go for it, and then suddenly it's twenty years later and they stop and look around them, thinking 'How did I get here?' and, more to the point 'Is this where I want to be?'

Some people, of course, do make plans and act on them quite early on in their life. They do all the research, talk to people, assess their own aptitude and then commit themselves to training for the job, only to realise six months into the job that it's really not for them. Some aspect of the job doesn't sit well with them, even though in terms of skills and aptitudes there's a good fit, and then they know they can't stay. Perhaps the culture or ethics of the company feels uncomfortable.

Others make plans and are successful and fulfilled in a job for many years, even build a career out of it, and then get to a point when they want something different. They've changed and the job doesn't hold the appeal that it did. Often this is around reassessing lifestyle or values.

Often people come to me for career support, embarrassed that they've reached a point where they seem to have changed their minds and want to turn their back on something that they were successful in. Others feel embarrassed that they never really seemed to know what they wanted. Sometimes people in their early twenties are concerned that their plans are already not turning out in the way that they had hoped.

So plans are a mixed blessing. They can provide a focus and help to define what we want, but they can also bring disappointments because of expectations. What if the reality doesn't turn out the same way as the plans? What's the point in having plans? Might it be better not to have plans at all?

Some people enjoy having plans and other people find them constraining. I'm one of the former - I feel more in control if I believe that I have a framework for life which means that I know what I'm dealing with. Having said that, I've lived on this planet for long enough to know that control is often an illusion and I'm just living with a belief that I have a handle on life and those I interact with - it's not reality. People in the latter category, non-planners, like to go with the flow and delay making plans until the last minute, acutely aware of their own resourcefulness to take up opportunities as they arise. My niece, Rachel, though similar to me in many respects, is totally unlike me in this, and when I hesitantly suggest that she might consider putting a structure together for her way forward in life, she'll say 'Don't use the P word!'

Limbo is different, though. In my experience of dealing with different types of people it seems to be the case that, planner or not, nobody likes a limbo state. I guess that if you're a planner you dislike the open-endedness of your current state, desperate to pull some boundaries around you, and if you're a go-with-the-flow type then you can't see where the opportunities for using your resourcefulness are going to be coming from.

Many people embark upon career change with varying degrees of confidence, some getting clarity on the way forward and some going as far as resigning, then they find that they are in a limbo state with nothing really tangible shaping up. Jobs might appear on the horizon but they don't quite hit the spot, they're not exactly what was envisaged in making a change. Sometimes the only jobs which seem to come up are similar to those which they've just left and they feel that they are being knocked back to do something they don't want to do.

So then it's that feeling of 'Why did I bother trying to go for it? It's not happening for me and I might have been better off staying put, not trying'.

Part of this is about identity. When we have plans which we're moving to fulfil we're throwing down the gauntlet to life by saying 'This is what I am. This is what's important to me. This is what I stand for'. When we're in limbo we begin to believe that maybe we don't really know ourselves after all.

We have to remember that we're always moving on, though. Just like the John Lennon quote, life is happening anyway. So, even in limbo we're moving towards something. We just have to find a way of getting through it.

Ways to deal with the limbo state:

- Use it as another opportunity to learn about yourself. Take it as a review time to consolidate what you know to be your strengths and weaknesses.
- Use your strengths to counteract your weaknesses to help you get through it.
- Be open to opportunities. Play with ideas. In the limbo state you've got nothing to lose.
- Build contacts. Opportunities come through people, so keep finding ways of talking to people about the way you're heading. Opportunities may unfold and while you're talking to others, you're refining your ideas.
- Keep contact with positive and optimistic people.
- Remind yourself of your past successes and disappointments and consider what you've learned through those. You've come a long way, baby!

PORTFOLIO CAREERS

'There are many ways of going forward, but only one way of standing still'

Franklin D Roosevelt (1882- 1945), past-President of the USA, generally recognised as the leader most responsible for mobilising democratic energies.

Picture this. I took my first HR role at age 33 following three years in University and a prior 13 years in shop work. My first day in corporate life comprised a quick induction with my manager, the HR Director, and then a baptism of fire straight into a two-hour strategy meeting with him and his direct reports (it wasn't so much that he was into baptisms of fire per se, it was more that he was so laid-back that he figured everyone else must be, too, so there was no doubt that I couldn't handle this. Gulp. By 10:30 I was already dizzy).

Anyway, I quickly found that I was asking for translations for the HR jargon. Fortunately for me, my new boss was patient enough to translate every ten minutes or so, but it soon made me realise that this was truly another world which I was entering (one of the actions from that meeting was to compile a glossary for the staff handbook, since they realised that not everyone, particularly new recruits, spoke their language) and I have to say that experience has given me a healthy respect for jargon.

So now, many years later, I sit here and I want to talk to you about portfolio careers. For those of you with prior experience of conversations about career, this is likely to be a comment which has its physical equivalent in water off a duck's back, but, given that earlier experience, I'm aware that for many of you there will be a question mark hanging in the air right now.

Portfolio careers. What's that all about, then? For an artist, a portfolio is a means of bringing together a diverse array of creative outputs. As far as careers go, it's the same idea: a collection of diverse ways of earning a living.

Many clients come to me with thoughts about their future career direction and want help in deciding a way to choose between options. A typical conversation might go ' I can't decide between going for a similar role in another big company or going freelance and, just to confuse things, I've just been offered secretaryship of my local squash club, which is quite appealing'. When I suggest that they may not need to choose, that it might be worth considering doing them all, they are often surprised.

I think that there's this idea of 'Jack of all Trades; Master of None' which means that anyone doing more than one thing can't be that good at anything. But let's look at it properly.

So many more people are approaching this way of working. Yet I still encounter a sceptical response which suggest that this is not a real way of going about career. The view is that surely nobody really chooses this, do they? Surely it's a second-best or short-term approach for those who are struggling to get a 'real' job or are just downright indecisive.

Actually, no. For those people who are clear about the diversity of skills which they have acquired, this can be a great way of earning a living, as well as fitting in some non-paid work, if you choose. To combine different skills and attributes, drawing upon different prior experiences, makes a lot of sense. Following several years' work experience under your belt and subsequent awareness of the richness and variety that is you, why should you shoe-horn yourself into just one of those aspects?

Many people think that portfolio careers are for those at the end of their career, just picking and choosing bits and pieces of work – combinations of employed, self-employed and voluntary roles – to tide them over until they slip into retirement, but for many people experiencing increased frequency of redundancy (three or four times during a career is not unheard of now) it becomes a more attractive option. They, understandably, become reluctant to put all their career eggs in one basket, and a portfolio career can be a way of gaining control over one's career without entirely relinquishing the benefits of employment.

Besides which, it can be a way of satisfying a need to do work which is 'valued' or 'worthwhile', according to your particular set of values, yet which does not pay very well, with work which is more financially rewarding yet not so personally satisfying.

But, clients say, the job I've applied for is full-time, so it's got to be a choice of one thing or another - doing both isn't an option.

Is that so? I wouldn't discount the possibility. If you get to job offer stage and it's apparent that your interviewer is keen, there's always the option to negotiate this. If you have a strong track record, many employers will be prepared to employ you on a part-time basis. They get the obvious benefit of lower salary cost and part-timers are often more productive, ensuring that they are focused on delivery; you would benefit from drawing upon the richness of your other life to bring to your role.

More people are finding the value of discovering a core set of skills and expressing them through different routes. The variety of approach is so appealing, and maximises opportunity for further learning. And this is a way in which many of us can consider our career options. Not just people who are at the top of the hierarchy. Not just people approaching retirement. People who know they have different ways of contributing and want to explore some flexibility in their job.

Think about it:

- Think about the options which you are facing and evaluate each one carefully.
- Think about the different ways you'd describe yourself - eg, marketing specialist, writer, community support, swimming enthusiast
- Which are important for a satisfying life for you and how can you better fulfil these?
- Be clear about your strengths, skills and most importantly, successes in each option
- Get feedback from others and be realistic - not everyone is comfortable with juggling different aspects of career.

TRANSFERABLE SKILLS

'It's no good looking after the pigs for thirty years and then deciding to be a ballet dancer, because by then pigs will be your style'

Quentin Crisp (1908-1999), flamboyant writer, actor and homosexual rights campaigner.

No-one is born as a tax specialist within the charity sector; a sales manager within the energy sector; a research scientist within the cosmetics industry or a career coach specialising in retail, for that matter. Our experience, education, aptitude and disposition shape us, over the years, to fit particular roles and build expertise, often in particular industries or sectors.

Once we get a foothold within these we build up even greater experience and carve out a track record for success, and frequently we become known for that specialism in that sector. So far, so sensible.

But sometimes, as our career and life experiences evolve, we want something different. We want to move out of this niche which we've defined for ourselves through training and experience, to use our skills and expertise in a different way or a different sector. This can often be something I see with older clients who've 'been there, done that, got the t-shirt' and want to offer their skills in a new context.

Career professionals talk confidently about transferable skills – how skills translate from one situation to another. But many people I work with have encountered difficulty in attempting to move from one sector to another. It is neither automatic nor easy.

In fact, some clients encounter huge problems in even securing a conversation to talk about it. Organisations and recruitment agencies won't even give them the time of day, and even if they haven't come across the Quentin Crisp quote above, you get a sense that thoughts akin to pigs and ballet dancers are pretty much front of mind.

We can be totally convinced that our offering can easily transfer to different environments, and it is possible. I come across many examples of people who've moved out, on and up. But it's not always easy, so how do we convince others that we can transfer our skills?

Now here's a recent case in point – Clive Woodward. To him, the idea of transferring coaching skills from the world of rugby to that of football was no big deal. But he had to go into print in the national press to state his case. With his back against the wall, he did what a lot of us do – blamed his parents. 'Honest, guv', he went 'Football is my true love, really, this rugby stuff was all circumstantial, it was what my dad wanted for me and I didn't have a choice. Then I became good at it and the rest is history...'

We don't all have the luxury (or mixed blessing) of the ear of the media, so when we want to state our case for transferability it takes a lot more effort, and our track record of success is not so apparent (but hey, looking at it another way, our near misses aren't there for all the world to see, either).

So what's the best approach?

I struck up conversations with fellow career coaches, recruiters and managers, and these are the messages which come through if you're looking for a change:

- First of all, understand the market/sector which you are trying to enter. If there are more applicants than jobs available then the recruiters hold the cards and it will be significantly harder to even have a meaningful conversation about it. So be realistic and prepared for a hard task ahead or a long wait.

- Accept that the more conservative sectors, such as the civil service, are more likely to resist the idea of transferring, while more creative areas such as the media might be more open to suggestions. This is a generalisation, though, and it depends on the recruiting manager, so take the trouble to find out what you can about him or her, and how open they might be to taking on someone not steeped in their industry.

- Recognise that you will need to be far more thorough in your research of the organisation and the industry – you simply will not be able to take as much for granted in an unfamiliar environment and your potential recruiters will, understandably, want to probe very hard to check that you really understand any differences, since you have no direct experience to draw upon. Truly get to grips with the issues in that industry and do some hard and specific thinking about how you would address those.

- Similarly, talk to people to understand how the skills which you have used elsewhere get played out in their industry. What's the same? What's different? Where would you need to adapt? How would you bridge the gap?

- Be client-focused. This is not about you, much as this move might be your burning desire – get a strong case together for how you can benefit the industry. Put yourself in the recruiter's shoes and challenge your case – or better still, get someone else to challenge you.

- Write your CV in such a way that the focus is on skills and not the job/industry/sector. A functional CV (see next section for the detail on this) works well in this situation, where you're emphasising personal skills and achievements, so a potential employer's eye is not so much drawn to the particular sector where you have gained experience. The focus here is squarely on you and your attributes.

- In the same vein, draw upon examples from a breadth of situations – socially as well as at work – where you may have used different skills. Examples might be in leading a team or managing accounts for an interest group.

- And if, at this stage, your list is looking a little light, then be proactive in getting some of these skills. After all, if you haven't got the skills or experience you think will transfer, why are you so sure that you can do it?

- Be convincing. Show passion and enthusiasm for the work which you believe you can do. You'll need an energetic approach to get up to speed if you're successful in getting that job, so you may as well start now.

- Show adaptability. Think of examples of where you've made changes in your life and have learned new skills and overcome obstacles. Tenacity, drive, a flexible approach and a positive attitude are all essential when you're going through change.

- Give the impression that you focus on outcomes, not processes. Processes and systems may be industry-specific, whereas most people can relate to conversations about achievements and results. Have up your sleeve some examples which demonstrate that you are flexible in approach and have adapted methods to suit situations – show that you don't have just one way of going about things.

- Use your contacts. I always speak about the importance of networking and, guess what, it applies here, too. If you have a champion who can recommend you that counts for a great deal. An introduction and endorsement of the way in which you operate takes away some of the risk for the recruiter. Have referees at the ready.

- Be flexible and realistic. You might have decided that you want to do a particular role in a particular sector but accept that you may have to spend some time in a different role first – to move sideways before you can move up. That has implications for salary expectations, too, of course, so be realistic about that, as well.

- Get feedback. If you're not successful initially, don't automatically assume that the recruiter is a plonker. Embark upon a dialogue to explore your strengths, shortcomings and approach, and learn from it.

GOALS

I was discussing life goals with my friend Michael. One of my goals is to own my house outright before I reach 50 – not so long to go now, and the chances of achieving that are beginning to look pretty slim, even to an unbridled optimist like me. Michael, who is not given to flannel, calmly told me that I could achieve it within a month.

'Like…..how?'

'If you sold your house and bought one in Australia, you could buy it outright now'

Okay, so moving to the other side of the planet didn't really feature in my short-term plans (or long-term ones, come to that), but it got me thinking.

How narrow-minded I'd been! I'd seen my goal as owning THIS house in THIS country. It doesn't have to be either, and Michael's right - if I really want to achieve that goal right now, it's more than possible.

How often do we pat ourselves on the back for setting goals and then later wonder why we don't achieve them. Frequently it's because we determine exactly how they are going to be achieved and what the outcome is going to look like and we become blinkered to anything which falls outside the way we've envisaged it. We smile indulgently at five-year-old girls who exactly describe their future husband in glorious detail, but really, do we operate so differently as adults?

The key is, when we set a goal, to think about what it is about it that makes it meaningful for us, and then to be open to other ways of getting the same results, perhaps through other routes. So for me and the house issue, it really isn't about this house, much as I love it. The heart of that goal is about having a base which will give me flexibility in supporting the lifestyle I want - some work; more writing; more travel.

A couple of weeks ago, I heard about a study which demonstrated a correlation between self-assessed luckiness - ie people who generally consider themselves to be lucky - and the personality traits of high extraversion, high openness and low anxiety. Not a surprise, perhaps. The study presented individuals with the same real-life scenario, but those who considered themselves to be lucky spotted the opportunities and took them, and received tangible benefits for doing so. Whereas those who didn't consider themselves to be lucky completely missed what was right in front of their eyes. If we learned to be more open and expressive and less anxious then perhaps we'd be 'luckier' in achieving our goals. I know for a fact that this has been true for me in the three years since I set up Ad astra.

How often, too, do we hear of people who've related how they've achieved a goal, but not at all in the way in which they'd expected. A 'chance' meeting with someone, the necessity to work around a personal crisis, the onset of illness - meant that they were deflected from the path which they'd originally mapped out, but they nevertheless realised, years later, that they had, in fact, achieved their goal, just not in the way they'd anticipated.

Don't misunderstand me, though - I don't equate openness with lack of focus. The two are entirely different. I make a distinction with clients between good intentions, broad aims and specific goals.

You'll recognise good intentions as the stuff of which New Year's resolutions are made. 'I'm really going to lose weight…' Broad aims are more of this nature: 'I'm going to cut down on the junk food I eat and exercise more.' Specific goals can easily be recognised as: ' I've joined the gym and will go for an hour three times a week; I've adopted a diet plan in which I aim to lose 6 lbs in the first fortnight and achieve my target weight in 4 months'.

When you set specific goals, then you make a commitment, and that is the crucial element in all this. It's about getting the balance between being clear and precise about setting goals, and making that commitment, but not being rigid. Having set your goals, it's about being open to opportunities and, most of all, relaxing into the process of learning about yourself on the way to achieving them.

If you don't set goals but just adopt good intentions, you'll never take those steps towards achieving something worthwhile - you'll never begin the journey. But if you keep fixed on specific outcomes in minute detail, you won't appreciate the journey and you won't be open to new experiences, new learning and meeting interesting new people along the way. Plus, of course, being open to exciting new goals which supersede your original one.

SECTION 3

'The job search scene has changed since I was last looking – how do I approach it and market myself effectively?'

WHO ARE YOU?

I've never been one to avidly follow current affairs but I'm always drawn to local news items on the TV. I think it's something about the skewed perspective it gives, which ranks wholesale death, destruction and corruption world-wide, as well as ground-breaking innovation and discovery, on a par with the news that a cat was stuck up a tree for four hours before being rescued.

So it was that I was watching the local news the other day and up came an item about a serious fire two villages away from mine. A local resident was interviewed. 'Ooh, that's John!' I thought, recognising him as a manager from my corporate career. But, what's this? Though I recalled John as being a senior professional in his field, a good manager, a stickler for detail, loyal and with a neat sense of humour, he was simply depicted as 'neighbour'.

I often reflect on the way that whole lives and personalities are thus distilled into one noun. Andy Warhol claimed that we all get fifteen minutes of fame and I've often wondered how my fifteen minutes of fame will mark me out for posterity – as 'onlooker', 'survivor', 'daughter', 'motorist' – whatever it is, it won't describe all that I'm about - there's more to me than one word! (Close friends will despair of my analysis into just one word, but will nevertheless, not be surprised).

Self-image is important – we will often go to a good deal of trouble to ensure that people see us in the way in which we want to be seen. It's not just about behaviour – what we <u>do</u>, which is what the news items concentrate on – but it's what we <u>are</u>.

This, of course, has relevance to careers. As a career coach, I'm not just helping people to find work – I'm helping them to define and make sense of what they are all about and the role which they fulfil in life, as expressed primarily through work. So when they come to describe themselves, it's a big deal. Firstly, in the sense that they need to feel that they are described accurately; secondly, because they need to feel comfortable with it. The first doesn't presuppose the second – it's about emotional, as well as intellectual, acceptance.

This is important on a CV or covering letter, where the way in which an individual describes himself or herself sets the scene in the reader's mind and paves the way for the next step – a conversation or interview. It probably has even greater importance for networking conversations – how individuals describe themselves on meeting new people.

Apart from that, it's important in those early conversations with me, where an individual is beginning to make sense of themselves in the context of their career. Before they even start to consider their direction, they need to be clear about how they see themselves. This is crucial, particularly when they have been made redundant or have had unhappy work experiences. In this case, they are questioning who they are and how much their contributions are valued.

And of course, it's not just a present focus – how they see themselves now – but how they want to be seen going forward. It's about future potential as well as current reality.

Some recent research into identity for those making the move from corporate life into an independent career highlighted that there is some tension between 'daring to be different' and 'acceptance by others'. This isn't, of course, confined to those who work as independent consultants, I'd say that a question on most people's minds when they consider any move towards a new role is about getting that balance between having something individual and distinctive to offer and fitting in with what's already there.

Most people who've been out of work for a while or desperate to make a move tend to focus on the latter – 'how can I convince them that I'm like them?' – rather than the former, but you ignore your own distinct personality, values and identity at your peril – if there is a huge chasm between the two then after the honeymoon period is over you'll wonder how you ever managed to think you'd fit! Then of course you'll spend a good deal of time and emotional energy extracting yourself from the situation.

This brings me to the Personal Profile. You know, that bit at the beginning of the CV which describes you in a couple of sentences. Some recruitment agents don't like them but I'm a great fan. Having looked at thousands of CVs in my earlier HR role, I appreciate a summary which can really give a flavour of the individual - not just what they do, but who they are. I begin to see the person behind the tasks.

They are not easy to write, though, especially good ones which are saying something meaningful. My advice is to leave the personal profile until the CV is finished then step back and see what picture is emerging – consider the themes and most salient points and pull those together in a brief summary which paints a picture of you.

Give it some thought. Instead of just writing a throwaway description which is based on what you've been doing – that is, lifted from your current or last job description, think about how you are comfortable with being described. You might have been in a managerial role, but perhaps you don't want to continue with the emphasis on management. So you might more comfortably describe yourself in terms of your specialist expertise.

This also applies to verbal communication, too. In fact, I would suggest that, before you decide how you are going to describe yourself on paper, you practise describing yourself in person. Summarise where your key strengths lie and what you have to offer. If it sounds hollow and unconvincing, then that's a sign that your heart's not in it. Work at it until you feel comfortable, even if it's a little vague. You'll find that you refine your thoughts as you express them out loud. As you become more comfortable, your confidence will build.

THE ULTIMATE CV

'Without continual growth and progress, such words as improvement, achievement and success have no meaning.'

Benjamin Franklin (1706-1790), scientist, inventor, statesman, printer, philosopher, musician and economist.

Your attitude to your CV is a bit like your attitude to your car. You can consider it as something to get you from A to B, or you can consider it as an item which reflects your personality and values and therefore as something to be nurtured and maintained.

I can already hear some of you saying 'Errr, what if I don't even have a CV?' I'll come back to you lot later.

If you view your CV simply as a means to an end, then you probably have the type of CV which is a list of jobs, qualifications and training courses, possibly every job you've ever had and maybe every school attended and every exam taken. What's wrong with that, you might think. Isn't that what it should be?

Well, you can view it like that, but you're missing a trick if you do, and, if your CV is just a series of lists, then to return to the car analogy, you're certainly not maximising all that power under the bonnet.

A CV is a marketing tool, which provides information about you - your achievements, skills and personality. It's a document which should make the reader think 'I'd like to meet this person. I want to find out more.' It's a means of getting people interested in you, and therefore a taster.

On that basis, you might already see that you don't need to list everything there is to know about you. You just need edited highlights. Primarily, highlights on what that particular reader might be interested in. So that's another thing - you'll need to take a look at your CV each time you send it out. It needs to be revised and revamped with the particular reader in mind.

So, one thing you need to do for sure is to think about it.

Now then, the big question. Does size matter? There are varying debates about the optimum length of a CV. Some people say two pages absolute max; other views are that for IT bods (who may need to list a string of software/ hardware/languages/systems) and scientific types (who may need to list research papers) that three pages is a more practical minimum. The key thing is relevance. Again, keep in mind the reader and what they want to know. Not what you might want to tell them, that's different; what they need to know in order to decide whether a meeting with you is worthwhile. If it's a taster, designed to encourage a meeting with you, much of the detail can be saved for the meeting.

Also, if you keep it top line, the higher the likelihood is of your being able to create an opportunity for matching your experience with their particular needs - make it too specific and you'll paint yourself into a corner; you'll be seen as someone only able to operate within a narrow range.

Don't let your CV get bogged down in lists of grades for exams, these have less and less relevance the greater the distance between today's date and your 23rd birthday. That word again - relevance. Educational achievements have greater relevance for a recent college leaver than for someone who's been working for a decade or more. The latter will have a track record of experiences to draw upon, which will supersede exam results.

Similarly, you don't need to list every job you've had. If you have had lots, there are ways of describing and summarising them to maintain the energy and momentum of the document.

Above all, think impact - be positive and direct. Talk about achievements, not tasks. Give a flavour of HOW you've achieved things - the skills which you've employed, the constraints and demands of the role, what the results were. A CV is not a job description and shouldn't read like one. Rounding it out in this way will bring your CV to life, and yes, even in doing this it is still possible to keep it to two pages.

Now, back to those who don't have a CV. Everyone needs a CV. You may be blissfully happy in your work at the moment, with not a thought to looking for your next role, but that's not the point.

A CV is a means of tracking your progress through a career, or different careers, so that it tells a story about you. Keeping it up to date prompts you to think about the next chapter. Where's this story leading? So when you look at it (which I suggest my clients do at least once every six months) you can consider it in the light of the following questions - What's the next natural step? What might you need to achieve in order to secure that next natural step, in terms of training or experience? Who are the key people you need to build relationships with?

A good CV keeps you focused and energised. If it's punctuated with achievements as I suggest then it is a way of reminding yourself of your success stories (and if you're struggling to think of recent ones then doesn't that, in itself, tell you something?). A good CV is far more than a document which describes the past - it should be a prompt for an action plan to take you towards your future.

CV tips:

- Keep it simple - limit the variations in style, fonts etc
- Think RELEVANCE
- Go for impact - write about your achievements and successes
- Don't use jargon
- Keep the tone upbeat and positive
- Ask yourself (or preferably someone else) - Does this document make me want to meet this person?

The chronological CV is the traditional format, and one which is most easily recognised – career history is listed in order of date with the last job first. The advantages of this type of CV is that it's easy to track your career progress so it's most useful when, in career terms, you want to do more of the same in the future. It reflects a picture of steady progression so if you've been building experience and getting regular promotions it's all there to see. It tells a coherent and predictable story-so-far.

Recruitment agencies, and recruiters in general, tend to prefer this type of CV since it doesn't require too much brainwork to see what you've done and when – any gaps or oddities would be readily apparent because your history is clearly tracked in a logical way.

However, just because this format prompts an approach based on listing past jobs, beware that you don't fall into the trap of simply listing tasks from previous job descriptions – that's pretty uninteresting. Make sure that you also give a flavour of how you've achieved tasks and what skills have been required. You still need to think about what is going to be relevant to the reader, so you may well need to fine tune the final CV by bringing some items to the fore and ditching others, to make your experience more interesting to the reader in question. Some sharp editing comes in really useful here – if you think you might be reluctant to ditch some info, get an unbiased perspective from a friend.

Training and qualifications are always useful to list, especially if they are recent – beware of listing a leadership course that date back to the

60s. Relevance is also important here too, of course, so just think about what will be meaningful to the reader. O-levels? Unlikely. Last year's self-funded computer skills evening class? – probably.

I personally like to see something of interests and hobbies as when I'm interviewing people it rounds out the picture of them as a person, which is part of what you're trying to achieve with your CV, but if you run out of space you may wish to leave out this information.

Similarly, you don't need to put personal data such as age, marital status, state of health (who is going to say that they have anything other than good health anyway?). A CV is a marketing tool, the aim of which is to secure you a conversation. The requirement for detail will come later, should you be offered a job, so don't fret that you'll have missed your opportunity to provide it.

Definite no-nos are photographs, coloured paper, fancy fonts, more than two fonts or formatting styles and dodgy hobbies (use your judgment).

SALLY ENDICOTT

2 Box Lane, Swindon, Wiltshire SN1 66U
Tel: 01793 784992 e-mail: sally@emailaddress.net

Training professional with over twenty years' experience of supporting personal development at all levels, with particular experience within the banking sector.

Skills and experience include:
- Positive and practical personal style, operating confidently and effectively in a variety of environments and situations, ranging from group work with retail bank staff to one-to-one coaching with professionals and board level directors.
- Effective delivery of training and development experiences to corporate and private clients in a variety of business sectors and across different cultures.
- Extensive use of training tools for effective intervention
- High standard of written communication, evident in training materials, Web-based articles and newsletters.

CAREER HISTORY

Training Consultant   October 2002 to present
Self-employed. Recent achievements have included:
- Developed business over five years to deliver large-scale projects requiring use and management of associates.
- Regular speaker for training groups and local businesses on use of training interventions
- Design and delivery of training courses for line managers and finance professionals on financial as well as management skills, both across the UK and in Europe
- Diagnostic work in partnership with key clients to define development programmes.
- Copywriting and editing an 'introduction to finance for non-financial managers' column for a professional journal.

Training Manager   1999 to 2002
Bloggs Bank
- Established and developed a new role to create a training function for a large and diverse group of people, following a merger between two High Street banks. This included defining policy and approach to training, including methods of delivery to individuals and groups.
- Introduced a coaching and mentoring culture within the bank, with the aim of retaining middle managers. After a twelve-month period retention had improved by 8 per cent across this population.
- Commissioned and completed a £1.8million pound "Performance Management Programme".
- Innovative leader with extensive experience of commissioning and managing complex multi functional projects
- Created and led a team of training professionals, effectively flexing human and financial resources to address shifting business priorities at a time of intense and rapid change.

- Member of cross-functional management team responsible for defining and implementing leadership strategy for the post-merger organisation.

Various training roles within Bloggs, at various times with Regional responsibility for High Street outlets and Head Office, gaining regular promotion. 1989 to 1999
Key achievements were:
- Supported and advised on training issues through effective communication with a demanding customer population, combining empathy and emotional support on sensitive and personal issues with a clear educating and directive role in clarifying legal considerations.
- Developed a competency framework for the business which matched business needs in order to deliver goals.
- Leading a team of Training Managers to facilitate business re-organisations, developed business wide succession and development plans.
- Responsible for setting up and running with development academy for future managers
- Setting up of internal assessment centres & introducing behavioural performance indicators to each job role
- Evaluating and amending induction programmes for new Area Sales Managers
- Coaching programme put in place to increase the effectiveness of the ASM and increase representatives "In Call" performance

Earlier career in retail banking, following successful completion of management training programme.

QUALIFICATIONS
Bachelor of Science degree, single honours psychology, at University of Wales, College of Cardiff
Qualified in Training and Development skills through the ITD professional study scheme.

TRAINING
Extensive training and management skills training includes facilitation skills, presentation skills, leadership skills.
Trained to administer and interpret a range of psychometric tools, including Myers Briggs & Belbin analysis
to an advanced level
Internal Leadership Coaching
Team Building through Ropes
3 day residential course- Finance for non Finance professionals

MEMBERSHIP OF PROFESSIONAL BODIES
NLP Practitioner
Member of CIPD

INTERESTS
Regular attendee at the gym and enjoy scuba diving when I can; visiting art galleries and occasionally do landscape and portrait painting; watching films, theatre and all forms of dance.

The functional CV differs from the chronological CV in that it pulls out experiences to list them under skills headings. This gives you greater flexibility and control in what you want to present first. This is important because the greatest impact comes from the first half of the first page of any document – if you haven't captured the reader's interest by the time they are half-way down the first page, you can probably forget any chance of influencing them.

So, this style makes the functional CV most useful when you are seeking a move to a different career, to a different industry/sector or if you want your next job to have more of something you've done some while ago but maybe not so much of, or not at all, in your current job. It's also useful where you might be 'downshifting', that is seeking a job with less responsibility than you currently have.

With a functional CV you have greater flexibility in juggling around experiences to reflect the job which you're aiming for and the reader is less distracted by your current job description.

Watch that this flexibility, however, doesn't create a 'stream of consciousness' approach. Keep focused on the reader and what the key messages you wish to communicate are.

The focus, then, with this type of CV is the transferability of past experience – how you can flex your skills base in different environments, so if you're aiming to move out of your industry/sector, for example, make sure that the language you use isn't too industry specific. Keep it open so that it makes sense to someone from a different environment.

There are mixed views on the personal profile – some people see them as very contrived, so of little value. Personally, I like to see a summary of what the individual has to offer – it helps me to decide whether I want to read more. I also believe that it helps the author of the CV to obtain greater clarity for themselves about what they are seeking.

Mark Jones

2 Excalibur Close, Ealing, London
T: 020 000000 M: 07979 9000 Email: mjones@email.net

Personal Profile

A positive and self-reliant marketing manager with a track record in design and delivery of marketing programmes in both consumer and B2B markets in the financial marketplace, delivering measurable business results. Meticulous and determined with the ability to communicate sensitively with clients and colleagues at all levels.

Key Achievements

Marketing Communications

- Developed, implemented, and measured global marketing campaigns for consumer and industrial financial products.
- Implemented targeted direct marketing and email marketing campaigns including call centre and database management.
- Completed existing user upgrade campaign achieving 7% sales conversion.
- Assisted with organisation of global marketing communications activities within large organisations, representing a business unit or country team.
- Managed scope and production of promotional multi media projects in Europe and the USA.
- Contributed to cross-divisional sharing of expertise through representation on the Loan Products Division of the Bank's strategic initiative steering group.

Branding

- Managed creation of packaging and associated branding materials for consumer financial software product including ownership of brand guidelines, collaterals and copywriting.
- Coordinated product and packaging production process in the USA and UK (with language versions)
- Managed production of branded product including delivery of software packaging in eight languages and developing brand identity guidelines for international use

Relationship Marketing

- Responsible for maximising business development activities across the business to develop a deeper understanding of customers - benefiting internal cross functional teams, particularly bids and proposals teams.
- Enhanced capability to implement targeted relationship marketing programmes with customers.
- Assisted the creation of the optimum environment for sales interaction with customers.
- Implemented ABC software and sales tools programmes across Europe and USA regions.
- Led the design and delivery of highly successful strategy development; business planning; usability research programmes; test plans; as well as gap analysis for successful product development and the identification of highly productive potential business areas.
- Supported sales forces, building marketing plans to help them influence customers.

Events

- Full attendee management and registration process for UK and European

customer events.
- Responsible for software product demonstrations at global events.
- Full event support and registration for customer parties and VIP dinners at major events.
- Organised four day Business Development and Sales Conference in Spain for 250 people.

Customer Service
- Managed US and UK Call Centres, resolving customer service issues, maintenance of product manual and training for call centre operators
- Developed customer care initiatives throughout organisations, call centres and resellers.

Internal Marketing
- Integration of activities with corporate marketing groups, gaining their understanding and support for marketing programmes.
- Support for USA channel marketing group and retailers/reseller programmes.
- Increased awareness of customer service issues within internal organisation.

Supplier Management
- Agency briefing and management, overseeing project development to timescales and budgets.
- Worked with all agency types - from full service to event management – UK and global.

Education and training
- March 2004 – Team Leadership
- February 1999 – Strategic Influencing
- February 1998 – Marketing Financial Products

Career History	
July 2001 – Present	Marketing Programmes Manager – The Bank, Ealing
February 2000 – June 2001	Marketing Communications Manager – The Bank, Reigate
September 1996 – Feb 2000	Sales & Marketing Planner - Joe Bloggs' Bank, Cambridge

Qualifications	
October 1998 – October 1999	MA in Marketing – Dissertation Subject: Branding in Financial University of London Services
September 1994 – June 1998	Chartered Institute of Marketing Diploma in Marketing
Portville College	
September 1992 – June 1994	BTEC National Certificate in Business and Finance
Anytown Technical College	

References
Available on request.

THE TRUTH ABOUT OLDER
JOBSEEKERS

'Nobody grows old merely by living a number of years. We grow old by deserting our ideals. Years may wrinkle the skin, but to give up enthusiasm wrinkles the soul'

Samuel Ullman (1840-1924) , religious leader and poet

Another new year, another reminder that you're a year older. A question I'm frequently asked by clients is - 'Am I too old to change career? Interestingly enough, that question is almost as often asked by a mid 30-year old as it is by a mid 40- or mid 50- year old.

Partly, this is because at school we are encouraged to make a decision - THE decision - about career path, which will hold until retirement, and even though we all now know that the world of work has changed, the feelings of discomfort about 'changing tack' still hold. (What will my mother think? I was so committed to my chosen career then.)

Partly, through the world presented to us by the media, we are led to believe that success in work, as well as in love, life and fame, belongs almost exclusively to the young.

For some individuals I see, career change is not their choice. They are forced into career change through redundancy, because there is no longer a requirement for the career which they chose when they were bright young things. The question which these people pose, to follow the one above, is 'Seriously, though, if a prospective employer has in front of him an application from someone aged 28 and an application from someone aged 48 and redundant, they are going to go for the younger one, aren't they?'

Are they? The answer is no, not necessarily. Here's the truth - recruiters are keen on older candidates, as long as they can demonstrate that several years' work under their belt equates to several years' experience and learning. You know the idea - has he got 25 years' experience or 1 year's experience 25 times over?

When you're interviewing someone in their early twenties, what you have in front of you is potential - granted, sometimes bucketloads of it - but that's pretty much all you have. When you're interviewing older candidates, what you have in front of you are tangible skills and experience and a proven track record, as well as potential. This is a big advantage. For many companies, facing significant change and needing someone to hit the ground running, proven experience is undoubtedly a more attractive option than waiting several months to see if all that glorious potential in a bright young thing is actually there. The guesswork is minimised - what you see is what you get.

But recruiters can't take it for granted that all that is there - you do need to DEMONSTRATE that increased age has brought experience, a host of experience which others don't have; that it has also brought self-awareness and refined interpersonal skills; that it's brought an ability to evaluate situations in a considered way and, accordingly, to use your well-honed judgment to find appropriate solutions; an ability to be more objective about what's in front of you; and that all that together has resulted in a demonstrable ability to adapt your style to a variety of situations.

The saying is 'older, but wiser'. I guess that the above list equates to wisdom of a sort, although those of us over the age of 45 often feel that 'wisdom' suggests a lack of spontaneity so we shy away from admitting that we've learned anything at all in the first half of our life.

You also have to demonstrate energy - energy to rise to a challenge and to be enthusiastic about new ideas, and to share these with youngsters who are making their way up the ladder.

In addition to all this, older people have generally built up a network of useful contacts and can have greater levels of influence than younger candidates, so that's clearly an advantage, too.

Phew! (Pause while you reach for the Phyllosan)

What you need to do is to write your CV in a way which demonstrates the building of the above skills and experience. The most successful older candidates are those who can demonstrate progression, but if your past career doesn't read as flowing as you might wish, get help with your CV - there are ways of 'telling your story' to emphasise continued development.

- Review your career to date - think about the results you've achieved.
- Make sure that your CV reflects these.
- Be enthusiastic! Passion doesn't have to be the hallmark of youngsters, but so often it's seen that way.
- Demonstrate your flexibility - in personal style, in thinking, in approach.
- Show evidence of a readiness to learn.
- Use your experience to think through the issues and come up with solutions. Don't be constrained by job descriptions or precedent.

P.S: If you're a twenty-something and you've read this far, don't think that all this doesn't apply to you. Use this framework to drive your career so that when you reach middle age, you'll be satisfied that you've got the maximum out of your career so far, you're clear about where you're heading, and that you have the edge over your fellow-workers of whatever age.

TESTING, TESTING

'Life's challenges are not supposed to paralyse you, they're supposed to help you discover who you are'

Bernice Johnson Reagon (1942-), gospel singer and folklorist; activist and historian.

Psychometric tools. Something which companies use more and more in recruitment. Why? To make you jump through hoops? Because the HR person needs to find a way of getting some entertainment value out of their sad little job?

Surprisingly, no. Companies use psychometric tests because they believe that it will provide additional useful information to support recruitment decisions.

First, some facts. (And listen up, because then you'll be better informed than some of the people who actually use these things).

Psychometric means measuring mental processes. There are two types of psychometric tools -ability tests and personality questionnaires. The latter are not tests because there are no right or wrong answers, as there generally (though not always) are with the former.

Ability tests encompass verbal reasoning, analysing financial data/statistics, abstract reasoning. These are an indicator of how you process information - a measure of 'mental horsepower', if you like. These should be used when there is evidence to suggest that the factors being measured are important for the job. If you don't do well on these tests, it doesn't, of course, mean that you can't do the job, but it might mean that you would struggle with certain aspects of it. This might sound unfair, but if these are used properly, that is, where there is hard evidence which says that, for example, most people already doing the job got 70% of the questions right in 35 minutes and you've only achieved 10% right in the same time, then this is what it's saying - you might struggle.

What seems particularly unfair is when this is approached rigidly. This chapter was prompted by a client who was advised that he had been shortlisted for second interview, having demonstrated appropriate experience via his CV and achieved 'best ever' results on an IQ test at the first stage. He then took an ability test and didn't do well so was told that he was pulled from the shortlist. Such a rigid approach is unprofessional and short-sighted. If I were interviewing, I would have taken the opportunity to talk through the disappointing results, discover why this was and explore ways of supporting him in getting up to speed in the required skill area. Then decide if it's a goer or not.

I have no doubt that they were missing an opportunity by binning his application without exploring it further. Their loss, but it left him feeling angry and didn't show the company in a good light.

Personality-profiling. Personally, I love it! But I know that it scares people. They are afraid that it will reveal some dreadful characteristic, unknown even to themselves, which will prevent them from getting the job.

Companies are never looking for clones - honestly! The idea of using personality-profiling is to understand your particular style, approach and strengths.

Ethical use of personality questionnaires in recruitment is, again, to use the results as a basis for discussion, as a hypothesis to investigate likely ways of behaving in various work situations. I believe that strengths and weaknesses are the same thing - two sides of the same coin. A strength becomes a weakness when it's used inappropriately. So being strongly decisive is great, but if you're leading a team at a time of change, you may need to ensure that you are overt about including their input into your decisions, otherwise they might feel alienated.

So if I were interviewing, I might say something like 'This profile suggests someone who is a decisive and forceful leader - tell me about your leadership style'. The key then is to have plenty of examples to draw upon - where you've behaved as your profile suggests and when you've adapted.

You should always get feedback on any psychometric test which you've undertaken. It is unethical to be asked to complete something and not have a chance to explore the results, ideally, as I've said, as part of a discussion rather than one-way feedback. Sometimes it's difficult to build in time for this on the day, though, if interview schedules are tight. If that's the case you should get feedback at a later date.

You should also be clear about why it's being used and what they are looking for - don't be afraid to ask. The data is about you. YOU are the expert on you, so you should take every opportunity to contribute to the picture which is being built up about you.

Used properly, psychometrics can be useful to you as well as to your prospective employer. Developing self-awareness is the foundation for finding the right career. Psychometrics can really help in this, so welcome the opportunity to find out more about you.

Key tips:

- When you are invited to interview, check whether there will be any psychometrics used.
- Practice. If you'll be doing an ability test, do crosswords, word games etc. to help you to prepare. Invest in some test practice books, readily available.
- On the day, try to relax into the tests. Make sure that you understand what's required of you. If you're not sure, ask.
- If you need glasses to read, make sure you take them with you.
- Don't try to fudge personality questionnaires. There are usually built-in 'lie-detectors' and what's the point of being recruited as someone else? You're trying to sell you.
- Get feedback and learn from it. You'll be better equipped for next time.

THE INTERVIEW

'Elegance of language may not be in the power of all of us,
but simplicity and straightforwardness are. Be what you say,
and, within the rules of prudence, say what you are.'

Henry Alford (1810-1871), English Dean of Canterbury, poet
and translator

Okay, so you've got yourself a job interview. Maybe it's for a job that you're really keen on. Maybe it's an opportunity which just presented itself and you think you may as well follow it through.

Your partner and friends might tell you that you'll walk it. Maybe. You haven't had an interview for a while though, and you've heard some horror stories so, even though you don't admit it to others, you're actually a bit nervous of how to approach it. You shrug off the importance of going for an interview but somehow it seems to be a lot more important now that you're a successful exec in your thirties or forties than it was when you were going through the milkround interviews following your college experience all those years ago.

Let's face it, you've been on all those courses to enable you to increase your effectiveness in a whole variety of situations, you've read about emotional intelligence and other business fads, your current success is due to your finely-honed interpersonal skills, so an interview should be easy-peasy. Why do you feel so uncertain about it, then?

I think that we all have a view of job interviews as a test. We see it as something over which we have no control. We hear dreadful stories of where interviewers have made candidates squirm and suffer. But it needn't be like that, and a good interview isn't a test.

I know, I know. I can hear you saying 'Tell that to the interviewers!'

The context for a job interview is actually very simple. You and the interviewer have the same aim – to reach a decision about whether you are the right person for the job. Now this is the bit that people so often forget – that decision is not just in the hands of the interviewer. You need to weigh it up as much as they do. That's why it isn't a test. Of course they have to make a decision, but let's not forget that you do, too. Keep that in mind and it'll restore a sense of perspective.

The way to build confidence is approaching an interview (or any other networking meeting, for that matter) is to have an agenda. This should have two main headings, 1. Information which you need to know about them. Them being the organisation, the department, the culture, the context, the manager and oh yes, the job. 2. Information which they need to know about you. You being your skills, experience, values and ambitions, and anything else which you consider to be of relevance when you're considering a life-changing decision.

Be clear about what knowledge and information you need to have under both those headings when you leave the room at the end of the interview. Knowledge that will enable you to make a decision about accepting a job offer, should it come your way. Write it down so that you can refer to it. Some people don't think of doing that – back to the idea of a test, I guess. In an interview, you can take papers in with you, you know.

It follows, then that you'll need to do some thinking in advance. This sounds obvious, I know, but I also know of many intelligent people who don't do that.

In terms of point 1, you need to think about what knowledge you need to get about them. The way to do this is to review what knowledge you have already and identify the gaps. This means research and conversations and it means reading between the lines.

In terms of point 2, what you need to tell them, it's about thinking about what they are looking for and how you are able to supply that. Don't prepare a hypothetical list of attributes in the key areas they are seeking, e.g influencing skills, working in partnership, etc. Instead, get together a list of real-life examples which demonstrate your attributes. Write them in this format: What did I do? How did I do it? What were the results? That way you'll be focused on results (always a good idea when you're talking to a prospective employer). It's more effective to focus on real life achievements instead of trying to talk about how you would operate in some abstract situation. And, as an aside, it'll inject some confidence into what you're talking about.

This targeted preparation will contribute to making the interview a genuine dialogue and not a contrived question and answer session. It'll introduce some energy into the conversation and you'll sound more interesting and come across as an achiever. Talking in terms of real life examples will relax you – and the interviewer, too.

Approaching it in this way will discourage you from trying to second guess what they're after. You won't need to. Just concentrate on what you have to offer.

Fine tune your agenda and approach to the context. Find out who will be interviewing you and think about what they are looking for. The HR person is more likely to be trying to determine fundamental fit in the organisation, motivation, and to identify any show-stoppers; the line manager will want to determine the detail on your skills and experience but will also want to understand whether he or she can really work with you; if you get to final stage interview with a board level exec, he or she will probably want to know whether you are a good investment. So try to prepare your examples to make it easy for them to get answers to their questions.

If you approach it in this way, you'll be less likely to be left guessing how you stack up against what they're looking for.

And hey, at the end of the interview you can always ask them. In the spirit of a true dialogue, why leave the room guessing how you shape up to what they have in mind. Asking the question will leave them with the impression of someone focused, energetic and clear about what they want.

- Set an agenda for what you need to get out of the meeting
- Research the organisation thoroughly

- Evaluate the gaps in your knowledge – in terms of job, organisation, team, future.

- Review your CV and prepare examples which address what the organisation is seeking, particularly in the light of who will be interviewing you.

- Consider which are the key questions you need answered in order to reach a decision.

BE YOURSELF

'The Self is not something you find, it is something you create.'

Unknown

I can remember when it was my first day at a new school, I'd be nervously awaiting the hour when I needed to leave home and my mother would say to me, reassuringly 'Just be yourself and you'll be fine'.

In my mind, being myself was anything but fine. I was painfully shy and recall one time when we'd just moved from mid-Wales to Oxford. On my first day at school, a fascinated group of eleven-year-olds crowded round me and asked me to recite nursery rhymes, just for the delight of hearing my quirky Welsh accent. My cheeks burning with embarrassment and humiliation at being singled out in this way, I dutifully did what they requested, quietly resolving to drop my accent as soon as possible.

Then, I would have given anything else not to be myself, or, even better, to be a different 'me' – confident, relaxed and, above all, English!

But still we carry on that idea that 'being yourself' is somehow the secret to success in life and I hear myself repeating the mantra to clients who are preparing for interview. Of course being yourself is important, it's only by relaxing into yourself that you can show what you have to offer. And presumably you applied for the job because you believe you have something to offer, but often we feel that being yourself is not enough and not what the recruiter might be seeking. We're acutely aware of our flaws and afraid that they're going to show.

Many clients are genuinely concerned that if they show their true self then they won't get the job. They think that what they should be doing is to second guess what the organisation wants and to create that persona.

This is never more so than when they are asked to complete a personality questionnaire. They try to skew their responses so that they appear to be more of a team player, or a leader, or whatever, but really, what's the point of getting a job when the way to guarantee success is to carry through that false persona for every working day? New jobs can be stressful enough without adding a requirement to act out a personality which isn't really you.

No, if a company doesn't have the flexibility to accommodate different styles and if you're so far removed from what they are seeking that you need to adopt a different personality, then believe me, you're not the right person for the job and you're doing no-one, most of all yourself, any favours by trying to squeeze yourself into it. Adapting your style and behaviour is a different issue, and I'll come on to that in a moment.

What we need to accept is that we are all individuals and that it's our individuality which we bring to everything we undertake. And yes, this means that we have good points and not-so-good points, but that contributes to the richness of interaction with others and the ability for everyone to learn, so there's no point in trying to brush them under the carpet. We often talk about diversity in the workplace, thinking of the benefit of a mix of gender or race, but we overlook the benefits of diversity in terms of personality.

So, surprise! Recruiters might have an idea of team 'fit' but generally they are not seeking clones – balance in terms of style is recognised to be useful in groups.

A key thing to remember is that we don't operate in a vacuum and that the good and bad points of personal style only become good or bad depending on the context. So for example, if you are a strong decision-maker then there will be times when that will be a valuable asset but there will also be times when it might be better to hold back on a decision, to take your time and consult others. It depends on what you're dealing with. So, a key to interview preparation is to understand how you operate at different times – in crises, dealing with conflict, dealing with a performance issue, etc. and to provide examples of how you have behaved in different situations.

This is where you might need some input from others. You will probably be aware of the behaviour, but what you may not be so well tuned in to is how others interpret that. A huge learning point is that others often see us in a different way from how we see ourselves. So for example, we might see ourselves as decisive, but others, particularly those who are cautious, might view that behaviour as pushy. Don't be defensive about other perspectives - perception is reality - and you will score brownie points at interview if you can demonstrate that you've sought feedback and accept others' views (and, ideally, that you adapt your behaviour as a result).

So what does that mean for the idea of 'self'? If you've demonstrated that you have adapted, does that mean that you have changed and have lost touch with your 'true self'? No, I don't believe so. I think that we all have a core self which is at the heart of who we are but that we can flex behaviour around that for different situations. I strongly believe in the capacity of humans to adapt. If I didn't believe that, I wouldn't be doing the work I'm doing. But I also believe in self awareness as a key to success and taking a proactive approach to developing our own style.

At the heart of it all you need to understand your core self so that you can understand what you have to offer, what you value about yourself and where this might be valued elsewhere, and also to understand where you might need to make adjustments, either to make yourself more comfortable with the situation which you are in, or to enable you to move out of it to another one.

So the message is to understand yourself without denying aspects of yourself. Understand the elements which would feel uncomfortable to move away from and which ones you can flex.

Experiment with different behaviours in different situations. There's no reason why we have to go on repeating the same behaviours just because we always did. We don't have to be stuck, and adding to your repertoire of behaviours gives you flexibility to operate in a whole variety of situations. (For hints on changing behaviour, see the book on Emotional Intelligence meutioned in the bibliography).

So check it out. It's worth getting a personality profiling assessment for yourself (available through Ad astra's Web site – www.adastra-cm.com) and to look at it objectively, to see how others might view you. Get feedback from others as to how they see you. It wasn't until 25 years after that incident I outlined at the beginning that I truly realised that some of my personal qualities might actually be valued. Don't wait 25 years! Understand what you have to offer and use it to your advantage.

THE INTERNET AND JOB SEARCH

'Education is knowing where to go to find out what you need to know; and it's knowing how to use the information you get.'

William Feather (1889-1981), US sociologist, educator,
author and publisher

I don't have to tell you about the benefits of the internet – instant access to tons of information; the ability to tap into advice from a host of contacts ranging from illustrious worldwide experts in their field to some nerd operating from a shed in the bottom of the garden two miles down the road from you. Wonderful, huh?

I don't have to tell you about the drawbacks of the internet, either - instant access to tons of information; the ability to tap into advice from a host of contacts ranging from illustrious worldwide experts to some nerd ....

Yup, you get my drift. We have so much information at our fingertips that it can be quite mind-blowing. You can find out anything about anything within a click or two. That's the awesomeness of it all. That's also the frustration.

Me, I'm just a technophobe, but I love real-life applications. The internet has changed our lives. Some things give me that Alice in Wonderland feeling, and here is one of them:

My boyfriend, stuck on a train outside Reading on a Friday night, just before we were about to fly to the Grand Canyon for our hols, called to ask me to research the weather way out west so that we could make some informed decisions for packing appropriate clothes. I looked at a weather Web site which reported 66 degrees and windy and relayed that back. 'What does 66 degrees and windy mean, anyway', I asked? He then suggested that I tap into a Web cam for Arizona. And there, in real time, I saw people drinking cocktails and mooching about – in shorts and sleeveless t-shirts. Yo! The internet has taken the guesswork out of much of our lives – we can, and are expected to, know things accurately and immediately. And isn't it great!

Groovy, and at the same time you're thinking 'Hey this is powerful!', you're possibly also thinking 'Hey, this is scary!'

So what does this mean for careers? Hmmm? If you haven't changed job for twenty years or so, you need to tune in to this. The world is different!

Is your memory of job change popping out in your lunch break to register with agencies? After-work conversations in dark, secluded pubs with a contact of an ex-boss of an ex-colleague? Surreptitiously sneaking to reception every day to look at the jobs pages, under guise of 'checking out the latest corporate press campaign'? Huh?

That's mostly gone. No longer do we send off a CV and letter, after careful investigation, in our best handwriting, to a carefully targeted recipient. We can whiz off applications by e-mail anywhere across the globe to a nameless, faceless e-mail address. Now, if we are having thoughts about a new job or career, we can organise the whole thing from the comfort of our desks. We can research what's out there, tap into the vacancy bulletin boards and apply for oodles of jobs without moving from our seat and all within half an hour. Well, in theory we can. Ease of use varies, despite apparently slick programmes, and sometimes we can be trudging through treacle two hours later. But, that aside, we can apply for jobs fairly effortlessly.

So how do we manage this new environment?

If you use on-line recruitment agencies then use them in the same way as you would one on the High Street. Don't expect them to take responsibility for your life and career, or even to remember you. Do expect to do the chasing and tracking. Ask people in your industry (or prospective chosen industry) which on-line agencies have worked for them and go on recommendation.

It's easy to see what jobs are advertised, and it's easy to apply. The flipside of that, as I've suggested in the first paragraph, is that it's easy to apply. At a recent conference for career professionals, the complaint from HR people was that 'the internet has made it too easy for janitors to apply for CEO jobs'. Organisations and recruitment agencies get inundated with applications, many of which are inappropriate, but the drawbacks aren't just on the side of the recruiter. Your challenge is, knowing that your application will be one of many, how do you make sure that you stand out from the crowd?

To go back to William Feather's quotation, anyone can find the information. The trick is to use it.

First of all, consider whether you are applying appropriately. If it's all too easy to apply, it's tempting to reduce the time you take to consider whether this job is right for you down to a nanosecond. C'mon, work is an important aspect of your life. One of the top three most important aspects. Get serious. If you're not going to be in the position of complaining that a) you never get an interview even though you send out on average 300 applications per week or b) that you find you've taken a job that isn't really right for you, then give it some proper reflection time. Do me that favour, please.

Take time to consider what the job is all about. Frequently, jobs advertised on the Web have scanty supporting information so don't fire off an application until you are sure you're happy that you understand what it's all about. Find a phone number and call the organisation to talk to someone about it. Just because we're living in an electronic world doesn't mean that there aren't people out there to talk to. Well, okay sometimes it does mean that, but not exclusively, and if you can't get to speak to someone in a reasonable timeframe (say 24 hours) consider what type of organisation this might be. Do you really want to work there?

If you've done your research and you consider that you don't stand out from the crowd, then forget it. And by the way, be aware that you won't be the best person to judge this, so make a point of asking a well trusted and objective friend for their opinion.

Treat your CV and covering letter (yes, you DO still need one of those) as though you were sending them by surface mail. There are plenty of CV templates around but there are drawbacks to using them – you may find them difficult to amend at a later date and, in any case, it might not suit your particular 'story'.

Send a copy to yourself to check whether the formatting looks on receipt as it did when you pressed send. I have seen some glorious messes in this respect and really, it doesn't take a minute to check, so do it.

As with all aspects of the internet, use it to save time but take a reality check now and then to match it against what you're trying to achieve. Start with a checklist outlining what you want and what you have to offer. Keep referring to it and don't get sidetracked. If it feels remarkably easy, then be assured that you're doing something wrong.

The key is, before you launch yourself at the internet, prepare. This is at the heart of so much in job search and it applies here more than anywhere. Think about what you're looking for, what your needs are, research the organisation, etc . Prepare, prepare, prepare.

- Don't be lured by the apparent convenience of the internet – go through the same processes of considering whether you really want to apply.
- Give some thought as to how to re-format your CV each time you want to send it. The beauty of the electronic format is that you can add, subtract or re-order elements every time you apply for something, so make use of that facility – sensibly!
- Do a test send with your application or CV to make sure it is received the way you'd like it to be. Don't assume that it will be, without testing it.

- Consider ways in which your application can stand out from the hundreds. I'm not talking about gimmicks here, think more of how you can personalise it – using the recruiter's name, making reference to recent press articles about the organisation.

- All in all, apply intelligence! Convenience of use doesn't mean that you have to take a dumb approach.

BACK TO BASICS

When I was a teenager, I spent many happy hours undertaking the writing equivalent of doodling, by compiling Love/Hate lists, the like of which you see in Cosmopolitan or other such magazines.

As in: Claire Coldwell, bestselling writer and radio presenter (because of course this was in readiness for my impending and inevitable fame), disclose her loves and hates as - Loves: The moon; almonds in any form; autumn; Prog Rock; paella; paradox; flying.....Hates: macaroni cheese; drying my hair; being taken for granted; lack of basic manners...

Yes, the last item always figured. Lack of basic manners.

I'm generally a tolerant and patient type of person but even though I'm pretty easy going in many respects, lack of basic manners and courtesies gets my goat.

So I was interested to see this week that Marco Marcucci, the mayor of Viareggio, in Tuscany, has ordered a crackdown on 'inappropriate dress'. That is, he insists that bikinis (for women) and bare chests (for men) are to be kept to the beach. This follows 'years of putting up with people who simply do not know how to behave'. Good on you, Marco!

Don't get me wrong, I'm not advocating Olde English formality for the sake of it – a friend this week related an observation on a family who were ritualistic in their responses (albeit well-meaning) following chastisement – 'I'm so sorry'; 'Thank you'; 'You're welcome'; I love you'.….. which rather smacks of Stepford Wives.

No, what I'm referring to here is all about respect and an understanding of what's appropriate to the situation, rather than predetermined responses. We are social animals and we should recognise – and respect - the impact which we have upon other human beings in a variety of situations.

Sure, we can do just as we please, and that is a huge appeal in a postmodern/modern society, or whatever we are. We are at liberty to behave quite freely and we are encouraged to express ourselves in an individual way. Diversity and difference should be retained. That's fine, but the trick is really about knowing how to express our diversity and individualism at the same time as respecting others, which means reading the situation, and acting upon it, appropriately.

Okay, careers (since I'm not really here on a wider mission to pull the nation up by its bootstraps)....

Sometimes when people are convinced of what they have to offer and focused in getting their message across, whether at interview or at first meeting or just in a general exchange with business contacts, they can lose sight of some of the fundamentals of human interaction. I'll give you a few examples.

Frequently new contacts are surprised at the speed at which I get back to them. They leave a message and I reply as soon as I can. Duh! Not rocket science, is it, exactly? Yet people are surprised because so often they don't get a reply. Ever. I have had clients, on a first meeting, tell me that the BIG name in career management has yet to respond to them, and guess what, meanwhile, they are well down the track in working with me.

My thinking is, I might not be the biggest or most established in this business but if people leave a message I can reply. Not difficult. But it's apparent that not everyone thinks that way. I was chatting to a carpenter about this. He responded to my call for a quote – he alone, among four whom I'd called. His view was 'If you advertise, you should at least respond to a request for a quote'. Anyway, what's important is that I've secured business, competing with the Big Boys, simply because I've bothered to reply and begin a dialogue.

Another example. A high-flying consultant, coming in to a (first) business meeting with a senior executive from a large organisation, to discuss doing some top-level coaching with the Board, came in quoting a day rate which matches my annual holiday budget and wearing a designer suit – sassy! Top operator, huh? ....and also sporting sunglasses atop her head and chewing gum while she talked. Do you think she got the business?

And another. A client, devoted father, had been made redundant and was in the job search process. His home answerphone had a delightful message with his kids screeching an excited welcome message down the phone. Ah, bless! But if that top-level headhunter called what might he make of it, I wonder?.....

So what does that mean for you in the job search process? It means attend to the detail. It means think about how others are seeing you. It means be professional. It means consider other people's expectations of the interaction as well as your own preference for how to operate.

I'm the last person to preach about politically correct behaviour but what I know is that there are expectations for particular situations and if you don't give those due diligence, you will be seen as someone who is not serious about it. Plus, you'll be seen as someone who lacks flexibility if you give the impression that you can only operate in one way for absolutely every situation you encounter.

Many people, these days, have spells of work abroad. There are books and courses on offer, which help them to tune in to the prevailing culture of the country they'll be working in – the manners, etiquette and unwritten codes. Why do people invest in this kind of support? Why don't they just carry on doing their own thing? After all, they are inevitably people who have a track record of success, otherwise this opportunity wouldn't have come their way.

They invest in this kind of support because they know that an understanding of the culture and norms of the country which they are visiting will smooth the path in their dealings with colleagues and clients, make interaction easier, less stressful and more enjoyable, and go more than half way in building relationships with others – oh yes, and those things are important in securing success, particularly if you're hoping for a long term relationship.

People consider cultural factors in their dealings with those overseas, but overlook the fact that there are unwritten codes in this country, too, which will of course vary depending on who you're dealing with.

In tuning in to others' expectations, you are giving the message that you want to be part of their group, that you respect them and that you honour their codes. It all sounds a bit tribal, and maybe it is, but if it prevents you from being excluded, then it's worth it. At the very least, it'll allow you a close enough look to see whether you'd like to be part of their group or not. Don't prevent yourself from getting that opportunity, at least.

Sure, when you get to know someone, you may relax your style, chew gum, wear flip-flops, record your Gary Moore play-a-like message for your answerphone, if you think the relationship can take it, but just be careful about first impressions. Retain the 'me' elements of your life, but if there's a chance that they might clash with expectations in the business world – assuming that it's a world which you want a piece of - just make sure that they are quite separate. It's worth it.

Otherwise, as the quote at the beginning suggests, you'll be 'wet on the surface' without ever being part of the water.

STAYING POSITIVE

'I'd look at one of my stonecutters hammering away at the rock, perhaps a hundred times without as much as a crack showing in it. Yet at the hundred and first blow it would split in two, and I'd know it was not that blow that did it, but all that had gone before.'

Jacob A Riis (1849–1914), photographer, reformer

and crusader.

My mother said to me recently - 'I'm glad I'm not one of your clients!' I was making her write a list of ten positive aspects of a situation which was troubling her, and when she pleaded to be allowed only five, I wouldn't let her wriggle out of it. 'Ten, and we're not leaving this teashop until you're done'.

Part of my role is to help clients to think through in great depth the situation which they are in, and sometimes that process needs hard work and a good deal of persistence. So at the beginning of a client relationship, we can spend a lot of time and energy exploring EXACTLY what was satisfying or dissatisfying about this or that work role, what are the qualities which the client most values about him or herself, EXACTLY how others might see him or her, or how they might have dealt with a situation better.

When we've done all that and we understand what we're dealing with - past, present and future - then we begin to get together a great CV and define a strategy to move forward. Then I make them practice describing themselves and what they have to offer in a positive way until they are really comfortable with it.

To get to this point can take a long time, it can be hard work and can be emotionally draining for both of us. I'll often nag, cajole and challenge and I won't let them off the hook. When we get to where we need to be, the client will often smile, breathe a sigh of relief, relax, and clearly be feeling pretty pleased with their achievements.

At that point I'll smile back, say 'Well done' and often think to myself 'You think THAT was tough, that's the easy bit'.

Because the truth is, in a quest for a fulfilling career, the most difficult bit can be when you're clear what you have to offer, you're feeling positive, you have a brilliant CV, you're ready to fly and...........there seems to be nothing out there. You scour the jobs pages and that great job - or even a half-great job - doesn't appear. Not just for one week, but for weeks on end. People don't even want a conversation about how you could add value to their company. The recruitment agencies won't entertain putting your application forward for a job which isn't exclusively based on your past experience. Your friends are telling you that you're bringing in a lot of money so why do you want to move jobs?

You begin to question your own wisdom in thinking about a career or job change.

This is the hardest bit - keeping going when it's tough. And it is often very tough , for many people. I wish that I could wave a magic wand and create jobs for people. But I can't, and my clients are aware that they have to do it for themselves. And often it takes a long time.

What keeps you motivated in a situation like this? Above all, that you know that you have something special to offer and that the right environment in which to contribute your gifts really is out there somewhere. That the knowledge that to stay in the situation which you're moving from is creeping death - if you stay there indefinitely you will lose some vital spark which is you. That at the heart of it all, you need to be true to yourself.

Support yourself when things are tough:

- Maintain the momentum. Keep looking, keep applying, keep exploring ideas. Schedule in time to jobsearch every week, without fail.
- Write a list of your achievements - in work and outside. Keep adding to it. Remind yourself that you have been successful in the past and you will be again.
- Compile a file of positive feedback about you. Look at it regularly.
- Remind yourself of what's good about the situation you're in - there's always something.
- Make sure that you always sound positive, no matter what you're feeling inside. Create a positive environment around you - a positive attitude attracts success.

- Avoid friends or family who are not supportive of your plans. You know the negative aspects of the situation, you don't need to be reminded.

- Keep networking - with old and new contacts. The more people who know that you're on the lookout for something else, the sooner you'll find it.

- Build in time for fun and leisure - recharge your batteries. If you've been doing all the above, you'll have deserved it.

WHAT REALLY COUNTS

'What lies behind us and what lies before us are small matters compared to what lies within us. And when we bring what is within us out into the world, miracles happen.'

Henry David Thoreau (1817-1862), author, lecturer,

opposer of slavery.

One of the most rewarding aspects of helping people to find satisfaction in their career is when I hear that ex-clients have made further moves to even greater success. It means that they are really beginning to manage their career for themselves.

So I was delighted when Paula called me to tell me about another career move. A chance meeting had led to an offer of a new job with big challenges and a high profile. Understandably, she was excited and thrilled, and she could see how her last two work experiences had led to her being offered this opportunity.

When we met up ten days later, however, the excitement had been replaced by fear and panic. 'I'm not sure that I can do this job – it's too big a stretch'. I pointed out that the recruiting manager obviously considered she could do it. 'Yes, but she didn't check my technical ability, she seemed more concerned about whether I'd fit with the team and had the energy to grow the business. I think she's made a big mistake'.

The reality is, though, that yes, technical skills matter, but other things can matter more.

Many people shy away from applying for jobs when they are not certain of their technical ability to deliver, yet we often hear of people who seem to be lightweight on technical prowess, yet who are doing a great job and are in line for promotion. How does this happen? Cynics might suggest that it's down to a well-developed ability to bluff or being well-connected in high places.

Generally, no. For one thing, there's more to doing a job than possessing tangible, technical, time-served skills and for another, technical skills can be learned far more easily than non-technical ones. So they're easier to train when you're on board.

Non-technical skills - those around relationships, approach to work and pure old-fashioned commonsense, can really oil the wheels and make a big difference to getting results.

This is becoming increasingly important as the work environment is changing. There's greater emphasis on relationships, which might mean working with different teams for different projects and working in partnership with external suppliers to achieve a common goal; a requirement to deliver more - and sooner - often means a focus on expediency rather than on meticulous detail; increased technology means that back-room jobs are now automated so that there's an emphasis on customer-facing roles. Someone who can manage this lot with a degree of success is, quite frankly, worth more than their weight in gold.

Coincidentally, when Paula and I met up, I had just been sent an issue of SHE magazine, in which I'd contributed to a feature entitled 'Impress More, Work Less'. The feature was not about promoting laziness or developing the flannel factor to a high degree of perfection, it was about maximising the impression you give at work through understanding yourself and those around you and playing to your strengths. Common sense, really.

A look through the magazine feature suggested to me three key themes emerging – efficiency, relationships and impact. I've provided a brief summary of them for you below.

Some time ago, I was at a conference where the psychologist from Big Brother provided us with parallels between success in the Big Brother house and success in business. No surprise that the most successful people are those who build genuine alliances with others, contribute to creating a positive atmosphere and who make themselves indispensable - regardless of whether or not they demonstrate leadership qualities. If we witness it in the rarefied atmosphere of the Big Brother house, then we know it must be true for real life.

So it's recognising that work these days is as much about how you manage the context as it is about what qualifications may be listed on your CV. Make sure that prospective employers are fully aware of both.

Work less, impress more:

- Invest time in building relationships with colleagues - Rob Yeung, business psychologist
- Draw on the expertise of colleagues - Jenny Cooke, teacher
- Set deadlines which make you look more efficient - Cliff Arnall, psychologist
- Communicate your achievements - Katy Nicholson, recruitment consultant
- Be tuned in to office politics - John Lees, author
- Network appropriately - Claire Coldwell, career management consultant
- Build your schedule around your energy cycles - Nick Williams, career coach
- Drive impact through non-verbal communication - Lesley Everett, author
- Speak and act with confidence - Ingrid Brindle, image consultant

NETWORKING

For most people I come across in the course of my work, the idea of networking is something which doesn't exactly fill them with delight. It's not British, after all. It's seen as being pushy, but worse than that, superficial - everyone can see through those meetings where interest is feigned in order to steer the conversation towards the subject of a job. Actually, I wouldn't advocate those kinds of conversations, but what I know for sure is that networking makes a huge difference in getting the job you want - whether it's a move to another company, promotion within your current company, or securing that key contract.

70% of jobs are not advertised. 70%! Surprising, but true. So all the jobs advertised in newspapers, journals, through agencies and via the internet only represent 30% of all jobs available. If this is so, how do people get those unadvertised jobs? Through having a conversation with the right person, that's how. Of course you don't always know who the right person is - neither does he or she until the conversation begins. Many jobs which don't currently exist are hatched through exploratory conversations. In other words, you can co-create just the job for you simply by having a conversation about your skills and the perceived business need. It does happen - I've done it myself and many of my clients give me examples of this.

So, if networking is so powerful, why are people uncomfortable with the idea of it? I think it's because it suggests that there's an in-group and an out-group, and that networking is about getting into an in-group. And you're not sure that you really want to be in it anyway, but it might be necessary in order to get you what you want. It also has connotations about 'using' people - a means to an end. Very few people like playing those kinds of games, and most people don't want to be associated with it.

Good networking shouldn't be - and isn't - like that. Good networking is just about having plenty of contacts to draw on for different purposes - advice, ideas, information, support. Perhaps different contacts for each. And you never know when you're going to need any of these, so it's worth maintaining those contacts, whether you're currently seeking a job or not.

This is particularly important with recent changes in the way in which we go about doing work - for example, increases in home-working, matrix management and shorter periods of job tenure. People can no longer rely on established relationships within an organisation as a means of logging and promoting their successes, ambitions and achievements.

Work relationships are much more fluid and the upshot is that the only person you can truly rely upon to champion you is you!

First of all, you need to be sure what you have to offer and know what you want. This can be the hardest bit for some people. Practise describing yourself and your skills in three minutes. Often, I ask people to do this in career coaching sessions, and frequently what they come out with is a summary of their current job description. That's not it. Think about you - what your achievements are and how you add value in what you do - your unique selling point.

And believe it! Be passionate and enthusiastic about what you have to offer. If you believe in yourself it's easy to be enthusiastic, and that's when networking is not superficial. A recent Harvard Business Review states that 20% of success is due to credentials and 80% to self-belief.

Approach networking with the idea of sharing information in mind, rather than the idea that this must lead to a job. Think about what you can learn and what you can share - that will ensure that you are talking to the right people. A friend of mine is fond of saying 'When you are interested, then you are interesting' and that's true. People will remember you and want to maintain contact with you if you are genuinely interested in what they are doing and what's important to them. Follow up your conversations by sending them articles which may interest them, or put them in touch with other contacts who might be useful to them.

Tune in to the personal style of the person to whom you are speaking. If they have a no-nonsense, factual approach, try to reflect that in the way you come across. This will build rapport more quickly and they'll feel more comfortable with you.

Specifically, don't ask for a job, even if you'd like one! This can be embarrassing for both of you, and is a sure way to guarantee a brief relationship. So keep in mind that you are seeking advice, information, ideas or further contacts - reasons to keep the contact going. Plan, at the outset, what you are seeking from the person you will be talking to (so you'll have needed to have done some research on that individual). Be clear about how they can help you and about how you can help them.

If you do this, you are not likely to go for overkill on networking. One of my contacts, renowned for having good networking skills, advises that you approach an event with the idea of making just three new contacts - that's all. But three appropriate ones, following sound research. She then tells herself that once she's done that she can go home. Often she'll stay because she's enjoying herself so much by this time, but her approach means that networking doesn't turn into a chore.

- Keep in mind that people genuinely like to be helpful, so don't feel awkward about seeking advice.
- Prepare for your conversations by being clear about what you have to offer and how your contact can help.
- Be yourself, and don't lie.
- Listen! Don't think that you have to do all the talking.
- Make a point of maintaining your contacts, even though they don't appear to be fruitful at present.
- Find different ways of meeting others - don't just use the same avenues.
- View every meeting as an opportunity to present yourself favourably - you never know where it might lead.

THE FIRST HUNDRED DAYS

So, after months of searching, you've found a new job. If you're very fortunate, you're absolutely on cloud nine, because it's THE PERFECT JOB that you've been waiting for all your life. More likely though, you're pleased, but not on cloud nine, because for one thing you never really know it's the perfect job until you've been in it a while.

Many clients I work with are absolutely clear that their new job is not perfect. Sometimes people make a move to a new role just to extract themselves from a situation which they don't want to continue any longer, so the emphasis is on what they're moving from rather than what they're moving to. Sometimes the new job, while not ideal in itself for various reasons – salary, location, future opportunities – might well represent a stepping stone to something else: an opportunity to keep earning while they're looking around for a better move, at best. At worst, an expedient move which will serve a specific purpose.

Whichever scenario fits you, it can be tempting, especially if the job search process has taken far longer than anticipated, to breathe a sigh of relief and think 'Well at least I can relax for a while'. Sure, relax and enjoy a different pace and a new environment, but let's not be passive about our career – ever!

There are huge rewards for constantly evaluating career options and taking steps towards them – this is good career management. And before you groan, if you do it properly, it doesn't have to be hard work. It can even be enjoyable.

Good career management begins even before day one in your new job. Let's just do some thinking about it, and see how we can get the most out of it.

And for those of you who are not approaching a new job right at this moment, you can pay attention, too. By adopting the following, you can inject some new energy into the job you're in.

The first thing I say to clients who are approaching a new role is to think about 5 key things which they want to achieve in the first six to twelve months. As a prompt, think of the CV which you'll be sending out when you're ready to make the next move. What will it have on it that doesn't appear there now? It might be management experience, a new skill, international working, partnering with particular customers. What's on the CV will be personal to you and hopefully if you had prepared well for the interview which led to your appointment in this role, you'll have a fair idea about what it is.

Okay, keep that in mind, but before you gallop ahead with your grand plan for the future, a note on the present.

Understand, and embrace, the role which you've been employed to do right now. This might not be the perfect job, and you might be keen to move on quite quickly, but not at the expense of your current role, please. You won't believe the number of people I knew in my HR days who were so keen to get promotion, or to use the job as a means of building contacts, that they had absolutely no focus on the job which they were doing. This is not the way to impress, I can tell you. Get a grip on how you'll get results in your new role, put some energy into it and use it as a launch pad for the future.

Get known for something. (I do, of course, mean something positive. Mimicking those in charge might be an endearing characteristic in a three-year-old, but not in an adult serious about driving his or her career). Develop a signature approach. What's your niche offering? How can you add value to this business through your particular skills and experiences?

Who are the key players? You want to make your mark, but you need to get the measure of the environment first, and understand how relationships work in that environment. Get to know who's who in the organisation and who will help you to achieve what you need to. This is not about toadying or playing political games but really understanding who are the movers and shakers and listening to them and their perspectives. (Yes, it's a good idea to listen before you offer your own pearls of wisdom.) You may also want to find a mentor to support you more closely in your new role; someone who can help you to really drive learning out of your experiences.

Make connections with people – peers, colleagues, customers. Learn about what matters to them and think about how you can address their needs through your role. Others will see you as interested and you'll also get to know the political agendas, which is undoubtedly useful if you're keen to maximise your experience while you're working in this organisation and it may also, through networking, enhance your standing externally, too.

Be aware of your personal style, your strengths and weaknesses. What do you need to do more or less of to build effective relationships? Get feedback on how you've operated in the past and then think of your strengths in relation to the new role – you might need to flex different aspects of your personality to be successful here, depending on the culture of the business and the nature of your role.

Where are potential blocks? Again, use past experience to draw upon. For example, if you've always had a problem getting a boss's support, think about why that might be. Is it something about your style or the way in which you make requests? Get feedback, if it would help.

Understand where the opportunities are. Find out where the investment is going and think about how external factors, economic, technological and commercial, might affect the future of the business. Consider what that might mean for your department, and what changes might then occur. How then, would you need to shape your offering to address these issues?

Be interested in the business and its direction. Look at the bigger picture – find out how your role/department is viewed by others outside the team and outside the business. Read widely about the business and see it from an external point of view. Talk to and, above all, listen to people.

Again, apart from being beneficial right now, this will have a dual effect of building networks for the future, too. Think about how you can enhance others' perceptions of the business through actions you might take. Use gut feel as well as logic to build your picture – think widely and imaginatively.

What training might you need in order to do your current role? Use your investigations into future developments to inform this. You'll need to justify the expenditure in terms of benefits for the business and not just for you, though if you can't see any immediate benefit to the business for the new skills which you personally want, you might consider funding your own training outside work in order to get the skills you need. Now, there's a novel thought!

What are the key milestones? Set yourself objectives to review at the end of weeks 1, 2, 4, 8, 12 and ongoing. Not just for tasks, but for all the things I've outlined so far. Share them with your boss if you feel it would help. But build in flexibility, too, and be prepared to revisit your goals as you find out more about the business. Also consider how your goals fit in with those of the team – don't be so single-minded that you are in danger of alienating others on your path to your future.

Lastly, but quite importantly, think about what has potential to cause you stress - Meeting new people? Learning new tasks? Change in routine? Dealing with detail? Operating out of your comfort zone? All of these are likely to come to the fore in a new job, so make sure that you know where to go to recharge your batteries. Predict days/activities when your stress levels will be higher and plan in energy boosters at those times to redress the balance.

So, understand how you can do your job well, and think about the following:

- What do you have to offer in terms of skills and experience?
- Where can you truly add value in your current job and how can you make sure that people know about it?
- Where are the gaps in your skills and experience?
- How can you develop the role to take you towards the next job?
- What training and development do you need?
- What can you become known for?
- Who are the key players?
- What are the key milestones?
- What are your likely stressors and what strategy do you have for dealing with them?

Do this lot and you'll be a winner!

SECTION 4

'My situation means that I have to stay put in this job for a while – how do I make the best of it?

POLITICS AND CAREER

'It is better to follow your own life's mission (dharma), however imperfectly, than to assume the life mission of another person, however successfully'

Bhagavad Gita, epic Indian poem given by Lord Krishna prior to the great war at Kurukshetra.

I was once described as 'the least political person in the office', which was fine by me and probably just as fine for those who were political animals. Here was one person who they could happily ignore in their quest to influence the big players.

And, after all, the fact that I was quietly getting on with my job didn't mean that my contribution went unnoticed, did it?

Hmmmm. This is the problem with office politics. I would like to say that the hare and tortoise principle applies here and that political animals are seen through, not valued, don't get promoted any quicker and generally get their come-uppance, but sadly, that's not necessarily the case.

Life isn't always like the movies and sometimes the political animals get their come-uppance, but more often they do get the rewards - the salary, the promotion, the big car - yes, and the girl.

Now why am I bothering to write about something which you well know and don't need to be reminded of?

Office politics is a career issue, that's why. It is a career issue because the nature of being political is that often these people receive career advancement at the expense of our own. It's unjust and unfair but the reality is that we can work our socks off for years and hope that we get noticed, meanwhile we see our colleagues (for whom we've been supplying work, ideas and information) leapfrogging us and getting all the glory.

That's bad enough, but all too often the political animal who most affects us is our own boss. The one person who truly knows what we are capable of, and could champion us if he or she chose, is the one who is constantly elbowing us into the sidelines.

How do we cope with those people who are prepared to ride roughshod over others, using people - us - to do the work while they bask in the glory? How do we stop others from stealing all the limelight? Should we learn to play them at their own game? Or should we turn the other cheek and just get on with it, hoping that justice will be done in the end?

I can tell you that I've been agonising over those questions, and having done so for some days now I really have to conclude that there's only one answer.

Leave. Find a job where your talents are more likely to be appreciated. Sometimes you have to accept that things aren't going to change, certainly not quickly enough. Meanwhile you're getting more resentful and your career is becoming more and more stagnant.

Understand what politics is all about. It's not about work, getting results, profit margins, loyalty to the company, the work ethic generally or the good of the customer. Here's a definition which you might want to ponder on: Politics is a strife of interests masquerading as a contest of principles – the conduct of public affairs for private advantage.

Politicking is about ego.

That makes it short-termist and transitory. It gets results, sure, but for the short-term and for a focused few. Now that could be a route you want to go down, but my view is that it's not sustainable over the longer term. Anything short-termist and transitory is fragile (even if it might not appear so from the sidelines) and we've all seen people who align themselves to one seemingly powerful person and then become casualties when that person falls from grace.

So, if you can't stomach your contribution constantly being sidelined, find somewhere else where it will be appreciated. I often tell clients that careers are like relationships - c'mon, you know when you've been there too long, you don't need me to tell you, do you? You know when you get to the point when you realise that it's never going to change.

And, like relationships, at the heart of this is respect. If you feel that what you're offering is no longer respected, you know that the writing is on the wall.

So, while you're taking steps to secure a job in which you are valued, try to establish a more secure footing, so that when you move on, it's with self-respect.

Some tips for dealing with work politics:

- The key is to be sure of what you have to offer - your skills and contribution. Sometimes we lose sight of that when we're surrounded by politics because we become unsure of what's truly valued, so our confidence gets shaky. This is exactly what I was saying about the short-term and transitory stuff. Do some work on it and get feedback from those whose views you value.

- Develop a 'signature' or brand for yourself, built on what you have to offer. For example, you might be skilled at facilitating conversations between different parties; troubleshooting and problem-solving; delivering to deadlines every time without fail. Get clear on what's special about you.

- Make sure that key people are aware of this set of skills. As broad a set of people as possible - internal, external, specialists, generalists. Believe me, if you do this, I can promise that some of them will genuinely be able to see what you have to offer.

- Be objective, consistent and positive, and be seen to be all of those. Be true to yourself and don't get caught up with others' wrangles. Concentrate on what you need to deliver for yourself. Keep your standards high because this is for you.

- Take ownership. Easy to say, I know, but absolutely insist on your name being on reports, on presenting your findings, on people knowing what your contribution is. Be persistent about it. It's your career. It might not make for a smooth ride, but so what - you're set on a new direction anyway, you won't have to tolerate it for ever. And meanwhile you'll be sure that you're doing all you can to become recognised for what you have to give.

- Focus on your CV and what you need to include for your next move. Be clear about the three key achievements you want to see there and drive your energy to delivering those. Keep focused on the next role for you and it will make it easier to tolerate this one.

MISTAKES

Let me tell you about a time I had to face up to a mistake. Not only to admit it to myself but also to two people who were paying me for my competence, expertise and professionalism. For a fleeting moment, when I realised the error, I considered how I could avoid telling them. They wouldn't have noticed it in itself, but a key part of the work that followed wouldn't have made sense so, realistically, not telling them wasn't a sensible option. So I bit the bullet and said 'Actually before we go any further you should know that I've made a mistake'. They looked a mite surprised but otherwise unfazed. Then I talked about what I'd do to remedy it and we moved on. Crisis over!!

'We all make mistakes….' we are thus reassured when we make an error. But we hate it, don't we! Yes, yes, we know that mistakes are a fact of life and we know that often we get some crucial learning from having made a mistake, but we still dread making a mistake and even more so, dread admitting it.

(No more was this apparent than in preparing this chapter, which originally began without the first paragraph. I hesitated to admit to you - current clients, ex-clients, potential clients, friends and the world at large - that now and then I make a mistake...)

Why do we dread admitting it, if mistakes are so commonplace and inevitable? Making mistakes makes us feel stupid and knocks our self-image – even if, like me, there's no way you'd ever refer to yourself as a perfectionist. We like to think of ourselves as competent and in control and making mistakes confronts us with the fact that we're not – always.

I'm always amazed when I hear people talking about a situation where there's some dispute about whose fault something is. I hear them say 'It definitely wasn't me, because that's not the kind of mistake I make'. This fascinates and amuses me, because it's as near as one can get to saying 'I never make mistakes' without actually saying it. It sounds very grown-up, doesn't it? Very self-aware. I always want to follow it up with 'What kind of mistakes do you make, then?' but I know that might come across as cheeky, so I just gaze at them in awe. Me, I don't have any particular speciality when it comes to mistakes. I can make all kinds of mistakes, sometimes more than once. And I have a feeling that when I hit 80 there'll still be new ones!

Facing up to our self-image about being less-than-perfect is particularly tough in the workplace when we have been recruited to a particular role because of our assumed competence. In fact, it might have been verified through certificates or references, so we feel justified in taking home that salary each month. But of course a CV chock full of qualifications and a track record of success doesn't mean that we're never going to make a mistake. So somehow, when it happens, we feel exposed – this wasn't part of our plan!

Learning to deal with mistakes is one of the most important things we can learn in life. The way in which we react and the way we move forward will mark us out as people who deal with adversity in a mature way and will accelerate our personal development, building our character and shaping us for future challenges. This applies to work life as well as personal life.

Let's look at the technicalities. There are, of course, errors of fact and there are errors of judgment. We all make both types of mistake. Errors of fact are usually known immediately. By nature they tend to be clearly wrong. The problem is often not in the error itself but in the implications for having made it. So for example, if you budgeted too small an amount for a particular purpose – you either have to abandon the project or make up the difference somehow. Sometimes we make such mistakes through having been given false information, sometimes we make decisions based on assumptions, but it's usually immediately clear that the error has been made and that remedial action is needed.

Errors of judgment are a different kettle of fish. We see evidence of it all the time, in others' lives as well as our own. Richard Nixon, David Blunkett, Bill Clinton, to name but three, misjudged situations they found themselves in and the repercussions were far-reaching.

The difference here is that this is often part of complex situations, and often involves a high degree of subjectivity. Sometimes the error is only apparent in hindsight and is not in itself 'wrong' but part of some code of values. Frequently errors of judgement are only errors because of other events which unfolded, so it might be 'If I'd known that, I wouldn't have divulged that particular piece of information…'; 'If I'd been able to see into the future, I'd have realised that that course of action wasn't the best…'

But hey, this is life. We can't see into the future and we can't know everything. And people make these kinds of errors for all sorts of reasons - to protect self-image, protect those around them or to enhance gain or reduce loss. These areas of human life get very murky indeed and the implications can be far-reaching.

Just reading through this chapter, I've realised that the mistake which I outlined in the first paragraph was an error of fact, pure and simple. Not admitting it would have been an error of judgment and would have taken me into an entirely different league.

In career change, many people I see are afraid to make a move. Any move – upwards, downwards, sideways, out. Promotion, demotion, retraining, new industry, new team. 'What if it turns out to be a mistake?'

Get this. I can assure you that any move is not going to be an error of fact – categorically and objectively wrong. Bits of it may not be perfect in the context of what follows, but what I can tell you is that, by moving, you will learn and develop and therefore be better prepared for the next move. You reach a crossroads and you choose, and nothing is truly wrong – it just unfolds in a different way. The biggest mistake is inaction.

Handling mistakes with maturity can develop our creativity and robustness and provide the opportunity to reflect and learn. It demonstrates our ability to adapt. You can view it as a 'laboratory' where our essential self is tested, in order to undergo refinement. That sounds like a good way forward to me!

- Deal with mistakes immediately and decisively – that will mark you out as mature, even if you still don't have the right answer.
- Seek others' ideas, if necessary. You don't always have to have all the answers.
- Reflect on how the mistake happened and how you can avoid it happening again in future.
- If others are involved, share the learning with them. This will build confidence in you.
- Be clear about errors of fact and errors of judgement. Sometimes we can't know what the outcomes of our actions will be, so don't let that force you into inaction.

SEEING WITH NEW EYES

'The real act of discovery is not in finding new lands, but in seeing with new eyes'

Marcel Proust (1871-1922), novelist and translator.

My approach to life generally is pretty akin to that of Alice in Wonderland. I'm constantly in awe of the beauty, variety and sheer amazement of life as it unfolds before me; the richness of interaction with people and especially (and doing the work I do, I'm reminded of this every day) people's ability to adapt, change, refocus and recover, when faced with all sorts of experiences.

So when I have the good fortune to travel, it's the Alice in Wonderland experience quadrupled. More, Greater, Bigger, and above all New, New, New experiences.

And of course, this is why many people seek work abroad and why youngsters are keen to round out their experience-so-far with a gap year (and increasingly, those not so young - a good friend of mine who's in his early 60s has just embarked upon a year out). New experiences and having new encounters is very appealing. We know that we will be intrigued, challenged and entertained, simply by being somewhere different. And I think that many of us believe that, in the process, we will learn something new about ourselves.

That, of course, can be true, and I can remember spending many hours in corporate life interviewing recent graduates who were trying to convince me of what they'd learned from their gap year. Sometimes they were spectacularly unsuccessful in this. Why?

Because learning is more about a state of mind than miles travelled or stamps on the passport. And some of them had missed that crucial part of the equation. They considered that the more exotic the location name, the more that future employers would be impressed. It's not as simple as that. Learning, as Proust reminds us in the quote above, requires a response from the individual. It's not just about being there.

One of the most memorable and delightful experiences of a trip to Australia was getting to know, albeit briefly, Janenne, our guide on a hiking trip in the Northern Territory.

Janenne was aged 45, a hearty and adventurous Australian with a zest for life. And she has lived. Before doing tour guides around her beloved country she spent some years as a social worker with young male delinquents. Prior to that she supported her fiancé for years through cancer, until, when he finally recovered, he announced that he was ditching her for his nurse. That required a refocus of her expectations of life, for sure. She had spent her childhood and young adulthood brought up on a farm where it was quite clear that her brother, though not at all inclined and not suited to it, would inherit the farm, while she, for certain able and willing to manage a farm, would need to seek her fortune elsewhere. So she'd had her share of challenges, you could say.

Janenne, as I say, had lived. But she hadn't travelled extensively. She told me about a psychologist she had worked with when she was in the social worker role. This psychologist was thinking about taking time out to travel. When Janenne asked why, this person looked surprised, as though it was self-evident. It was about learning about life, she explained, learning about other people, about different perspectives. Janenne looked around at the boys in her charge, some drug-dependent at an early age and now recovering, some living with severe injuries, for example amputated limbs at age 18, most of them written off as no-hopers before they reached adulthood, and she thought that you could well tap into different perspectives and learning about life without leaving town, if you so chose. It was all here for the asking.

Don't get me wrong. There's nothing wrong with travelling. The key is to be open to experiences. But often people think that life-changing experiences will ONLY come through travelling and not be open to experiences closer to home. What Janenne had realised was that it's about state of mind rather than physical location. She told me that she learns more about other countries through interacting with her charges on the hiking tours than ever she would by travelling. And, seeing her in action, I believe it.

So it can be with your work. Sometimes circumstances mean that we have little choice but to stay where we are for longer than we might want to. We get itchy feet. We know that our destiny lies elsewhere and we feel that our wings have been clipped because we have to stay in the job when we know that there's a whole amazing world out there. But for financial reasons, or because we're undergoing training, or because we're supporting our partner, or for some other reason, we're obliged to sit tight for some months, perhaps even years.

Instead of champing at the bit, it can be more helpful just to relax into it and to think about what this situation is telling us and what we are learning about ourselves. It helps to approach it consciously so that we have a checklist of things we need to achieve in the current position. It could be to develop particular relationships, get a specific skill under our belt or have exposure to a particular experience.

I often mention the value of focusing on your CV and using it as a prompt for career experiences. So think about what needs to be on it which will stand you in good stead for your next role, then make sure that it happens. Write these things down and then you'll be committed to doing them instead of just viewing them as 'nice to do'. Create an action plan.

Think in terms of achievements, not tasks. Again, your CV will have greater impact if it gives the impression that you were getting results rather than just biding your time. You'll be viewed as someone who approaches life with a more proactive and positive attitude. Then when you do fly the nest, you'll be in a better position to take the learning that comes your way.

Consider:

- What are the good things about being here in this job at this time?
- How can I use my experience to best advantage – for me and for the organisation?
- What can I learn from others?

- What new skills can I learn to add value and to best equip me for a move, whenever that might be?
- What do I need to achieve before I can make the next career move?

LITTLE THINGS THAT MAKE
A BIG DIFFERENCE

'The little things are infinitely the most important'

Sir Arthur Conan Doyle (1859-1930), doctor, writer

and spiritualist.

Margaret, the Personnel Officer who was training me to take up the reins when she retired, was called to the warehouse to deal with a drunken member of staff. Margaret consulted the mirror which she kept in her desk drawer, always within arm's reach, checked her hair and carefully reapplied her lipstick, before turning to me with a 'How do I look?'

I was somewhat bemused, I have to admit. 'Errr, you look fine!.........'
'Ummm. Margaret, it's just a drunk!'

'I'm well aware of that! Standards, Claire, standards!'

Margaret was renowned for impeccable grooming. She was also known for visibility — HR could never be accused of being a faceless function while she was around.

She probably wasn't aware of it, since she didn't have much time for theorising, but she had what I've since recognised to be a 'signature presence', which, for her, was based around 'standards'. I recall that after she retired she came in to the office for a visit. She was horrified that my boss, the HR Director, was in casual dress. 'What if you're called to a meeting with the Chief Executive!' she exclaimed. He giggled and said, 'Margaret, he's dressed more casually than I am!'

Okay, old-fashioned or not, it's not a bad thing to have some characteristics which are distinctive to you, and to use them to your advantage. Sometimes it's tiny things which can set us apart from others — they work together to build an image of what we are all about, as individuals.

In fact, we all have a unique set of attributes, and psychologists would tell you that because of the huge number of contacts we make in the course of modern life, we have to very quickly find a way of making sense of the information we're presented with about others. We need to adopt a shorthand approach in our interactions, to quickly assess what others are all about –- friend or foe; supporter or antagonist. We assess and decide within minutes, based on pretty scant information, much of the time, and we build a picture from the few building blocks of information we are presented with, to create a 'reality'.

But we're not always aware of our own personal attributes, so it's useful to bring them to consciousness. If we do that we, at least, stand a chance of managing the 'reality' which others see.

I just read an article about Tom Cruise. He's a private person, but what IS known about him is that he's a nice guy. Rated so by journalists, fellow actors, taxi drivers, film directors, yes, and even ex-wives and ex-girlfriends have a hard time finding some real dirt to dish. The Sunday Times journalist writes 'He laughs easily, makes intense eye contact and can make an introductory handshake seem like an intimate connection.'

Hmmmmm. Yeahhh.

Oh, where was I? Yes, I was on the verge of saying that these are all small things in themselves, but build up to an overall picture of a personable guy.

And for Tom Cruise, are these natural or are they contrived? I'd say it doesn't matter where and how they originated, it's an image which is consistent and sustainable for him. A personable guy. No question.

So what does all this mean for you and for the job search process?

The key things I'm driving at here are - 1. Messages are transmitted; 2. Best take control, then; and 3. Be aware of the small ways in which you can do that.

We're aware that in the job market we can be competing with many others, and we need to find a way to set us apart, to develop our own 'signature presence'. And this is more than just the sum of our skills and experiences, it can be the way we market ourselves or the way we do things. Like a handshake or eye contact.

It can be about finding ways of doing something which is distinctive and that we'll be remembered for. So, okay, let's move away from Hollywood and star-struckness and get down to the nitty-gritty.

Being courteous and friendly to people you encounter on your way to the interview counts for a lot. So be friendly and cheerful to the receptionist. Make eye contact. Connect with them as people. Believe me, their opinion is often sought. Besides which, you can find out a good deal more about the company and its culture through ten minutes well-spent in reception than you can in a two-hour interview. Worth the effort.

Be positive. Positivity is an underrated attribute, but important. On balance, are you going to recruit someone to your team who stands a chance of making you feel better about life or a Victor Meldrew soundalike?

Let me tell you about a psychology experiment. Two sets of students were given a list of attributes of a visiting professor, which included such things as intelligent, articulate, energetic etc. There was only one difference – one list included the adjective 'warm' and the other 'cold'. On hearing the professor speak – same lecture exactly, the latter professor was given an overall negative rating and the former an overall positive one. We build correlations in pieces of data in a way which is objectively irrational, maybe, but as I said earlier, we want to make sense of the world, so we quickly move to an overall view.

If you're not naturally attuned to others and don't see yourself as gregarious and 'other-focused', then you need to develop your own signature presence which is focused on other attributes. For example, communicating in writing.

In this era of electronic communication, how distinctive do you think a paper CV appearing in the post is? Especially if it's printed on good quality paper? In fact, any documents sent by post will stand a chance of being more memorable than something which can be deleted with a click. We're not talking about bombarding people, but sending out something which has been thought through will make a difference.

Of course, negative little things can make a difference, too, so do your best to be aware of those. Not returning calls, a negative demeanour, poorly presented CVs, jibes at past employers – these all count against you. You'd better believe it! As someone who's spent many hours sitting the other side of the fence I despair at how or why people choose a job interview to explain in great detail how, in their view, their boss was a plonker at best and a criminal at worst.

These are hints for the short term. My approach to supporting people with career issues is to promote a view which is focused on developing a strategy for managing career for life, not just short-term bursts of activity.

The key to effective career management is to be working towards your next role at all times, not just when you are actively seeking a new role. That means ensuring that people are aware of what you are all about and what you have to offer, and the types of opportunities you are seeking in your next role. It's about building an image of who you are, so that when opportunities come up, you're front of mind with key decision-makers.

In terms of building contacts, clients often get war-weary when I tell them, yet again, that they should be maximising their contacts – networking. But here's a convincing argument in terms of little things making a big difference. In his book, The Tipping Point, Malcolm Gladwell talks about folding a piece of paper 50 times. How high does that reach? Most people say something like as high as a refrigerator or as high as a skyscraper. The answer is it takes you to the sun. And if you fold it one more time, of course, it goes to the sun and back again.

The point is that you get to a stage, then, where steady progression takes you into another league, and that's what we're talking about here. That doing something just one more time will make a sensational difference, so take a deep breath, make that phone call, research that company, just do it!

LIMITING OURSELVES

'It is our duty as men and women to proceed as though the limits of our abilities do not exist'

Pierre Teilhard de Chardin (1881 – 1955), Jesuit,

palaeontologist, biologist and philosopher.

Soon after I set up my career management business, I was asked to do a copywriting job. Copywriting? - that wasn't what I'd set out to do! But I thought about it (after all, someone was offering me money to do it) and I considered that, a - I had experience of, and opinions on, the subject in question, b - my writing style was pretty good, and c - thinking about doing it energised me, so as I began to turn the idea over in my head, the thought shifted from 'I can't do that!' to 'How can I do it?'

I began to realise that for years, in corporate life, I'd been constraining myself by my job description. Copywriting? Not me. Wrong person, wrong department. Of course, in an organisation you need to have clarity about roles and need to be sure that people are, at the very least, undertaking the job which they are being paid to do, but nevertheless we limit our achievements by creating rigid boundaries around what we are, and are not, willing to undertake.

So often we see ourselves in terms of what we do now and lose sight of the wider picture of what we are all about. We look at the tasks which we are required to undertake and the prescribed methods for doing them. We look at the limits of our expertise as defined by our job description. Then this becomes a self-fulfilling prophecy and we become that person constrained by those boundaries.

And, let's admit it, there's a level of comfort in that - we're fairly likely to succeed because we're operating in a safe zone.

However, being defined by our job description can turn into a truly depressing experience if the industry we are in is in decline, the writing's on the wall for our job role and we don't particularly feel an affinity with what we're doing anyway. We're in danger of losing confidence by associating ourselves too closely with what we're doing rather than with what we are. You won't believe how many people in this kind of situation say to me 'But I can't do anything else – this is what I am'. Frequently I hear this from teachers, for example, who believe that they are only able to operate in a specific way in a specific environment.

I recall that once, on a team-building day for the HR team I worked in, at an early part of the day we posted up on a wall chart all the HR achievements we had under our respective belts. There were some surprises. Several people said to me - 'I didn't know that you were an expert on job evaluation'. Well, why would they, it wasn't what I was doing at the time, but it turned out that it would have been useful for one guy to have known that because of a project he was working on.

Defining ourselves in a narrow way, focused on current job requirements, limits the way in which we are seen by others, but more importantly, limits the way in which we view ourselves. Because we then become unsure if we can do anything beyond the boundaries which we've set. Worse than that, we then limit our next career move to build on what we're doing now, a step-by-step approach, so we get even more entrenched in a rut. We also limit our opportunities for new experiences and learning.

We limit opportunities for those around us, too. If I believe that I can do elements of my boss's job, and he gives me the opportunity to do so, then it frees him to do a bigger role. Everyone benefits. The organisation benefits from having people push their boundaries forward, and everyone feels happier from being able to use their breadth of skills. We then prepare the ground for future experiences, to develop skills which we might need in future jobs.

The world of work is changing so rapidly that if we approach job change by building incrementally on our current experience, we are truly going to miss out. Those who are bolder in their aspirations will be there, ahead of the rest, taking the opportunities, stretching themselves, making an impact and very likely having a lot of fun.

Think about

- What are the skills and aptitudes which I'm using in my current role?
- What are the other things which people tell me that I'm good at?
- What skills was I known for at school?

- What am I convinced I'd be good at, if only I had the opportunity?
- Are there skills I use outside my work which I could apply in my job?
- What skills would I like to use in my next role?
- What stops me?

FOLLOW MY LEADER?

'Fix the problem, not the blame'

Japanese proverb

One of the most inspired casting decisions in recent movie history is that of Judi Dench as M in the Bond films. And one of the most memorable lines which she gets to deliver in that role, evenly and dispassionately, is '007, I will not tolerate insubordination'.

Insubordination - now there's a thing. What's that all about? Is it about old-fashioned values which don't really have a place in the cut-to-the-chase approach of modern life? Is it, in the Bond example (plus some real-life ones which come to mind, now I come to think of it) just about macho man versus power-dressed woman? Is M on a power trip? Is Bond? Or is it about the fact that MI6 is steeped in traditional structures which support hierarchy and have little time for practical expedience?

Hey, well, all those things are what make Bond films compelling watching, for sure, but is it just fiction or is there a place for some of these notions in real life?

Fast-forward a few years to 2005, small screen, Alan Sugar running (with thinly disguised delight), The Apprentice, a reality TV experience where two groups of Bright Young Things are set a tough business challenge. More in the way of compelling watching. When things go wrong, the team leader of the losing group has to nominate two team members to be sacked and Alan Sugar decides which one.

So we see a board meeting in which the team leader has to state her case for why success eluded her team. A fair dollop of antagonism ensues between the two female members of the team. Boy, I wish it weren't just women, but all too often it is.

There seems to have been an issue in the team member accepting orders from her leader. Alan Sugar (Whoops, Sir Alan, insubordination, remember!) takes a decision that the team member is the one to go and in subsequent conference with (who are those people – his PA and his butler? I missed the first few programmes and I've never quite understood their roles) he says 'You can't have it. If there's a leader you can't have bickering. They may not be right but they are the leader.'

He's right, of course. The leader is the leader, and we might not like his or her decisions. Come to that, we might not like him or her as a person very much, either, but they are still the leaders.

For those of you whose hackles are rising, I don't meant to suggest that a leader should never be challenged, that by virtue of their status they are automatically right in every decision they make and that they shouldn't be questioned. That's not it at all and I wouldn't subscribe to the view that title, or lack of it, and place in the structure brings with it automatic acceptance of one's lot.

For me, Sir Alan hit the nail on the head with this bit – the bickering. Bickering is never justifiable because it shifts the whole dynamic of the relationship away from something objective to something personal. And for Bond and M, for sure they were too well brought up to bicker, but M's point was that direct and personal challenge should be made in a particular environment, and that environment is not a public one.

What's this got to do with careers?

Quite a lot. Last week I spent a day with a group of graduate trainees exploring personality types. This was a group of people who each, to a man (joke!) plans to be a leader in the not-too-distant future. We spent some time considering leadership styles and they recognised that leadership isn't simply about telling other people what to do. That's one way of going about it, but it's not the only way and it is a style which has less currency these days and in most working environments than it used to.

The problem can be that when the chips are down, when you're under stress and you really have something to prove, it can seem that the only way to get results is to assert yourself; to draw upon the old autocratic style. People do this for a couple of reasons. One is that some people genuinely like bossing others around; the other is that it gets results. But often at a price.

What you need to weigh up is the long term versus the short term. You may get results today through issuing orders but people do like to feel valued, so if you are not recognising their contribution appropriately, you'll lose out over the longer term. They'll take their contribution elsewhere.

The key to work relationships (or any relationship, for that matter) is about having effective conversations.

As someone on the receiving end of instructions, you also have a responsibility not to get sucked into bickering and negative conversations. This can be particularly hard if a) you don't have much respect for your leader, b) you don't agree with what you're being asked to do and c) everyone else around you is having a gripe.

Add to this the fact that you are bright and ambitious and you will feel that it's only natural that you should point out the flaws in your boss's thinking and behaviour. But are you really going to score the brownie points you think you might be? It's doubtful. For one thing it only adds to an already stressed situation if you generate more negative stuff and for another, people don't forget it and it could mean that you are excluded from future opportunities because you're labelled as difficult.

One of the most valuable skills you can learn is to express yourself without being personal or aggressive. Get feedback, through personality profiling and/or asking others, to see how you might be viewed in this respect. You could be surprised. What you view as assertiveness may be seen by others as aggression.

It is, however, easy to do something about it. There are plenty of assertiveness training courses available as well as self-help books. Through personality-profiling, I have worked with people to adapt their interpersonal style. It's not about selling your soul or conforming at the expense of your own true nature – it's about understanding when different styles of expression are appropriate and using them to best effect.

So, if you're in a frustrating work relationship,

- consider if this situation if telling you more about you than about your boss.
- understand your own style and how you generally react to different personalities.
- learn to express yourself without being negative. There are ways of pointing out that there might be a better way of doing things, even to your boss.
- don't let it escalate into something nasty. If he or she won't listen, step back.
- if it really is a problem and your boss is truly unreasonable, chat to your HR department to make them aware of it.
- keep results-focused and look for win-win solutions. Get known for what you deliver, not for your cutting observations on others.
- build a reputation for being polite, rational and team-focused and able to work with anyone. Others will notice.
- model the behaviour of a leader whom you admire.
- find a (proper) outlet for your frustration and stress. Go to the gym, talk it over with your partner – get it out of your system.

Most people will accept feedback when it's delivered rationally. You may be unlucky, of course, and have a boss who doesn't tolerate any sort of feedback. If so, you may not see any changes while you're working for him or her but at least you'll be storing up information for yourself on how not to behave when you're a leader.

BACK TO WORK

'My education takes place during the holidays from Eton.'

Osbert Sitwell (1892 - 1969), English author

As I sit here typing, the field which I overlook is being ploughed, having been harvested last week. We're at the end of the summer and within a week the new school term will start. The summer holidays are over for most people, though some are making the most of the fact that parents with small children are back home, so are enjoying an early September break, away from it all.

Holidays – we love them. We also need them as an opportunity to recharge our batteries and prepare ourselves for the long winter months when life can seem that bit drearier.

How are you approaching your return to work? Is it a case of 'Don't ask me, I'm trying not to think about it', actively avoiding contact with anything that will connect even a small part of your brain to the world of work?

Or is it the case that you've never stopped thinking about it, making notes for that big presentation coming up, avidly reading the business pages in the papers and taking every opportunity to check e-mails and take calls from the office?

If you recognise either of these scenarios, chances are that your break wasn't all it could have been, both for you and for those with whom you spent your valuable leisure time. Putting your head in the sand (I am speaking figuratively here, of course) or behaving as though you're still in the office is not what your nearest and dearest deserve.

But it doesn't have to be all or nothing – a truly beneficial holiday is one where you come back rested and re-energised and ready to get back to work, and if you're really lucky, inspired with ideas.

Everyone needs a break, and never more so if you're not enjoying your job, if you're feeling put upon and taken advantage of, if the pressure is enormous and the hours are long and you've got to the stage where you're not enjoying your evenings and weekends – that's assuming that you're having any – if things are really bad it could be that you're working non-stop.

If you recognise any of this, though tempting just to crash out on a beach and not give work another thought until you need to get your suit out of the wardrobe, reluctantly, the night before you return to work, it can be a missed opportunity not to give a little brain space to it. 'Why? I'm on holiday!', you cry.

Because, if you don't give it any thought, you'll be back on that treadmill and feeling exactly the same when the next holiday comes around, so you won't have got the true benefit.

I'm not suggesting that you make use of your well-earned break to de-vote your time to analysis of your career strategy (or lack of it), but when you're in a relaxed frame of mind, away from all your usual everyday pressures, sometimes it's easier to get a perspective on where you are and, more importantly, what you could do to change things.

If your work situation is really bad, you might want to set aside a chunk of time to think about it and/or talk it through with your partner, but I'm not suggesting that you make a major exercise of it. There are tons of good career books on the market, but I'm not suggesting that you make those your holiday reading, either, unless you really have set yourself a target to take some long overdue action on this. Even if that's the case, though, I'd say leave your holiday alone and get the relaxation you need, but do schedule a couple of days for it when you return. I'm very keen on setting my clients homework, but even I recognise that there's a time and a place for it.

What I'm suggesting is that you keep alert to your situation – your thoughts and feelings, hopes and fears. Nothing heavy, it's just about tuning in to your perspective when you're relaxed. You may want to spend ten minutes every other day jotting down some notes, just to capture some ideas coming through.

It's more about keeping antennae out for your work perspective. So, for example, you meet some new people in the hotel bar. You get talking about work and tell them what you do. How did you find yourself describing your work? How did you describe your role? Were there some bits you emphasised and others you glossed over? Presuming your employer is not MI6, what does that tell you about your attitude to work?

Think about what you're doing on holiday and what you really enjoy. Are there aspects that really energise you, which you don't get in the workplace? For example, do you enjoy social aspects of your holiday - meeting new people - whereas you work in an isolated way with limited contact with others? Were you doing something creative on holiday whereas your work is quite routine? Or vice versa: Is your work a plate-spinning series of priority shifts whereas on holiday you slip into a totally predictable routine? Do you want more of these elements or is it something which you value simply because it happens on holiday and therefore represents time out? Think about it. Get a view.

When you're listening to others talk about what they do, are there elements which really appeal. Do you find yourself thinking 'Yes, **I** always wanted to do that, but never got around to it'?

You might find some themes emerging, some patterns taking shape. This is why it's useful to jot your thoughts down – suddenly ideas can connect in a way which you hadn't previously considered. It's also about control. If you are consciously evaluating your feelings and ideas about work it puts you much more in charge, even if – no, **especially if** – your work situation is an unsatisfactory experience for you.

Take all these thoughts a bit further and think of ways which you could have a more satisfying job. It might be about bringing in greater creativity to the job you do, making your boss aware of skills that you have which you don't use very often. It may be about exploring retraining. These are just thoughts, and I'm not suggesting that you frighten your partner and kids by announcing that you're going back home to hand in your notice and live on a canal boat, earning a living by making macramé bracelets, particularly if you've come to this conclusion after six Long Island Iced Teas and a heart-to-heart with Pedro the barman.

All I'm saying is explore these ideas because there might be some mileage in incorporating them into your life. I always tell clients that they are not making a commitment to anything until they sign a contract. You can go a long, long, long way into researching and exploring what else is out there without getting remotely near to a commitment. Try ideas on for size, see how you feel about them, share it with the family, have fun with it.

Many of you will be spending your holiday time with your teenage children in the last few weeks before they go to University or start their first job. You'll all be aware of this transition and the change to all your lives. You, as a sensible adult who's been through that transition, haphazardly or smoothly, but whatever – you did it – will realise the importance of the way in which they approach it. What's the advice which you're giving to them? I'll bet it's something like this: work hard, learn as much as you can about yourself, be yourself and have fun.

Are these things true for you as you approach your return to work? Take your own advice, see where there's leverage to get more out of your everyday life. That way, you'll get more out of your next holiday, too.

EIGHT STEPS TO CAREER SUCCESS

'We are what we repeatedly do. Excellence, then, is not an act, but a habit'

Aristotle(384-322BC), philosopher and scientist

In these empowered and enlightened days, employers proudly tell their staff to manage their own career development. However, most people are not properly equipped to do so and haven't a clue how to go about it. That's understandable, no-one was ever taught career management in schools, our parents were probably in the same company (if not the same job) from school until retirement, and if you ask around your peer group you get as many differing pieces of advice as you have friends.

So where do you begin?

Step 1 - Understand the concept of
career management.

Good news: gone are the days when we were made to feel nothing short of inadequate if we weren't crystal clear at age 14 of our career path for the rest of our working life. It's okay to change your mind - and your career. We used to view it as failure if people shifted career. Not any more, it's smart. Why? If you're changing career it probably means that you're adapting to a changing work environment, going with the flow, learning, reviewing how your own skills fit with the careers which are opening up.

The world looks a bit different from when we were at school: jobs - and companies - come and go. Employability is what you need to aspire to, not simply employment. So career management is not about knowing all the answers and having a career path mapped out, it's about adapting and being flexible so that you are best placed to respond to opportunities. Better still, the people who've really got this cracked learn to create their own opportunities. Read on...

Step 2 - Know yourself.

Self-awareness is the key to success. If you're clear about what you have to offer then you'll be clearer about what you can do. Take opportunities for feedback - learn to see yourself as others see you. Personality-profiling and 360-degree feedback can be invaluable in this. Seek objective professional assessment if you need to - it'll be money well spent. Be aware of ongoing changes in your self, your skills and what interests you.

Exploring your self will inevitably mean that you find yourself taking risks - pushing your personal boundaries forward - in order to find out what your skills really are and what you enjoy. Also consider your values and what motivates you and how these shape your sense of a satisfactory work experience. Understand your strengths and your pressure points - where do you go to recharge your batteries? What motivates and energises you? What are you known for in your organisation?

Also look at the bigger picture, at your lifestyle. What changes do you need to make to your work life to accommodate changes in your private life? If the two are not in tune you'll experience stress, so learn to anticipate change and deal with it.

STEP 3 - FOCUS ON SKILLS, NOT JOBS.

Jobs are changing rapidly and some jobs exist now which didn't a few years ago. It's also more difficult to determine exactly what people do - the title Marketing Manager, for example, can encompass an entirely different range of tasks in one company over another. Also job titles become redundant, whereas skills are transferable. So forget about job titles and concentrate on skills - that way you'll be flexible about new opportunities, either in your current organisation or in different industries. If you scan through vacancies with this approach, even you will be surprised at what you could do. Write your CV to focus on skills and achievements, not jobs.

Think about what you've achieved and how you did it, that way you'll build up a picture of your unique contribution to the work environment.

Step 4 - Set goals.

You can't get anywhere if you don't know where you're going. Come on, you know that's what you tell your children. Again, this is where focusing on skills has the advantage over focusing on job titles. Ideally set short- and long-term goals but concentrate on short-term ones if the future is just too fuzzy right now - it will unfold, I promise.

Be clear about how you want to build on your skills to secure the next job. Is it developing a specialism to build on your current expertise? Or is it developing new skills, eg experience of managing others, to move into an entirely different role? Set smart targets for achieving these goals and use your key strengths to support areas where you are less strong (this is why you really need to know yourself).

Step 5 - Know your industry.

Learn about what's happening in your industry. Read everything you can and think about the implications, not least for your own role. Understand the challenges facing your industry and think about the skills which you have which will address those. Also think about the skills which you don't have right now which you will need to acquire.

Be one step ahead. Join professional organisations. Become someone who is known for being tuned in to what is happening. Publish articles and conduct seminars to demonstrate your understanding. By becoming informed about your industry, you'll be the first to take advantage of new jobs and the first to spot when it's time to move on.

STEP 6 - KEEP LEARNING.

This will build on your self-awareness and increase what you have to offer, both within your current organisation and externally. As long as you're learning, no-one loses and everyone gains. On that basis, most companies will fund training which has some relevance to them. Recent training always looks good on your CV, especially as you get older - it suggests that you're still open to new ideas and ways of doing things. New skills and experiences broaden your options for work and, as an added bonus, make you a more interesting person.

STEP 7 - BUILD A NETWORK OF CONTACTS AND USE IT.

Most jobs aren't advertised. Make sure that people know of your current skills and future aspirations, so that you'll be front of mind when those to-die-for opportunities come up. Know what your contacts are interested in and supply it. Learn to network effectively, ie not a scattergun approach, but with a desire for genuine exchange of ideas and information with the right people.

Step 8 - Make time for regular reviews.

Well, how can you know if you're on target to achieve those goals you've set if you don't make time for reviews? Take a minimum of half a day every six months to review your career. Using your CV as a focus, think about what you've learned and what new experiences you've had. If none, why not? Think about what you need to do to move on to the next step. Then do it

SECTION 5

'There's more to life than work – what about the bigger picture?'

WORK-LIFE BALANCE

'When you do something meaningful, your capacity to replenish yourself is high.'

Doug Kruschke, management consultant, coach and facilitator.

How to achieve work-life balance is one of those modern dilemmas under constant debate. And one which I certainly haven't got right, if we think of balance in terms of proportion of time spent working as opposed to proportion of time spent doing other things.

For if you enjoy your work and find it fulfilling, as I do, then you inevitably spend lots of time doing it, reading about it, thinking about it and talking about it. Okay, I could exercise more and visit my mum more often but, truly, I wouldn't say that my life feels unbalanced even though I apportion lots of time for work stuff.

Am I deluding myself or is it just a matter of definition? Richard Reeves, in his book 'Happy Mondays', refers to a cartoon where an artist is snarling at his wife late at night, 'I'm not a workaholic! Lawyers and accountants are workaholics. Artists are DRIVEN!!'

This, surely, is the point - work/life balance is a subjective issue. One man's work is another man's recreation. So to agonise as to whether we, as a society, have got it right, is missing the point.

The work-life issue as it's usually portrayed is about allocation of time, and social commentators lament the fact that longer working hours are expected, and that people have no choice but to deliver. Actually, we have more choice these days about the hours we work, and statistics demonstrate that it is mostly the people who are able to choose who work longer hours. Work can be fulfilling and it's great if you love it.

Don't misunderstand me - I do recognise that there are issues, but I believe that they need to be considered at an individual level, not a societal one. I think that the true issues are as follows:

Issue 1 - Recognise when work is stressful. If your work is having a detrimental effect on you and those around you, then that needs to be dealt with. Look out for increased dependence on destressers (excessive alcohol consumption, overeating), increased irritability and a feeling of not being in control. If work is stressful or unfulfilling, look for another job. Yes, you! Don't accept a situation which is draining your energy - you deserve better.

Issue 2 - Recognise what's right in terms of work/life balance for you - and communicate it. This is a tough one. It can be hard to admit that you'd genuinely rather work than visit Auntie Vi. Ensure that those close to you understand what appropriate balance looks like for you and understand what it might look like from their perspective - talk about, and reconcile, the difference between the two.

Have honest conversations with your boss and co-workers, too. Make sure that they understand how work fits with the rest of your life. Live it, and then they'll respect it. But don't expect them to understand it if you haven't talked about it.

Issue 3 - Reframe the way you think about balance. The issue is not about rigidly dividing your time between elements of your life, but understanding what balance is. Balance isn't about opposites - it's about equilibrium. It's not about 'work' or 'leisure'; - some primitive cultures don't differentiate between the two as opposing concepts, and don't have words to express them in that way. Life for them incorporates aspects of each, interwoven.

If you believe that you're giving something of yourself to your work, then it's unrealistic to partition it off for expression in one arena. True balance is about eroding the boundaries so that work can be fun, creative, socially fulfilling, relaxing and inspiring in the same way that home can be about achieving goals, debating and negotiating effective utilisation of available resources and learning new skills. None of these belongs in one domain only.

Balance is about drawing upon different aspects of yourself in every situation you find yourself in. It's about experiencing the richness and variety of what life has to offer and allowing the enjoyment of that to be expressed in everything which you do. When you take steps towards achieving that, you feel energised.

Approaching life in this way gives us opportunity for self-expression and allows us to be seen as individuals, rather than in terms of the jobs which we do. That makes times of transition - change of job, retirement, even redundancy, easier to deal with because we have retained our sense of self.

And, as an aside, it also means that you're less likely to become boring. My sister, formerly Head of RE and Philosophy at a prestigious girls' school, told me that it was crucial that she kept up with Eastenders so that she could better illustrate discussions of moral dilemmas. Her perspective was broader (and more fun for her pupils) because she would just as soon quote Beppe DiMarco as Bertrand Russell or the Bible.

The main focus in achieving balance is about being tuned in to the different aspects of our life and how each affects the other. It is when this is out of kilter that conflict and stress have the potential to arise, not through working long hours.

- Stand back and take a view on how work fits into your life as a whole
- Are you energised by everything which you do?
- If you're not comfortable with what you see, find a way to redress the balance
- If you are comfortable, make sure that you build in regular stress monitoring
- Ensure that others understand how work fits into your life and how you want it to, for the future
- Seek variety in the activities you are involved in
- Enjoy!

WHAT'S SACRED TO YOU?

'The power of the heart aroused is enough to break down any limitation, any barrier and to overcome all obstacles'

Anon

On holiday one year (Hawaii, since you ask), I was chilling out at a full moon beach party which my friend John was hosting. John gathered the forty or so guests in a wide circle and asked us to each introduce ourselves to the group and to 'say what's sacred to you'.

There was a whole variety of responses, some predictable perhaps, for example, 'my children', 'the planet', some not so predictable, more individual. My friend Michael had said 'the sea' but I knew that, living and working a couple of hours' drive from the coast, he didn't get to see the sea too often, and it got me thinking about how what we value is not always translated into behaviour.

What does sacred mean, anyway? Regarded with reverence or respect; set apart; holy. Whichever dictionary you prefer, you'd probably agree that it means something special and important, that you hold as a highly valued part of your life and to me it also suggests something on which you won't readily compromise. I thought about the people who'd said that their children were sacred and wondered how many times they chose to stay at the office instead of going to the school Sports Day or Nativity Play. I thought about people who say they value the environment and wondered if they lived a pollutant-free life.

So are people telling lies when they state what's sacred and their behaviour doesn't follow through? I don't think so, I don't expect people to be perfect, and I'm not cynical about the idea of holding something sacred, either. Far from it. What this exercise highlighted for me is that people frequently have to make compromises which often result in squashing their values. Also, it made me think that people don't generally consider what's sacred to them until they're asked.

But we do always have choices and when we are publicly asked to state what's important to us we are reminded of those choices. And we can take opportunities to harmonise our values with the way we live our life. If we make our co-workers aware of what's important to us then it's easier to make choices in line with our values, for example to finish work in time to get home to read the children a bed-time story, or at lunchtime to switch the PC off and go out for a walk instead of working through. So we can get support in living our values simply by articulating what they are.

People appreciate a work environment which supports their values, so if you're a policy maker or a manager you'd do well to respect what's sacred for your employees. If you ask them to compromise too often, you might think they're happy to go on doing it, but they won't do it indefinitely. Your task as a senior manager is to find a way to build a bridge to the sacred elements in people's lives.

Ask yourself -

- What's sacred to me?
- Do others know about it? If not, why not?
- What in my life recharges my batteries?
- When was the last time I gave it quality time?
- How can I make it more a part of my life?

TAKE A BREAK!

'Where space is, there is being'

Friedrich Nietzsche (1844-1900), philosopher and poet

Proofreading a newsletter for an organisation for career professionals, I came across the following: Claire Coldwell is President of the West of England and Wales Chapter, UK Board secretary and, as UK President-Elect, a member of the World Council. She runs her own consultancy, Ad astra.....

'Gosh', I thought to myself, 'you're pretty active'.

'Twas not always thus.

I recalled that, long ago in corporate life, I had asked for feedback from one of my internal customers. Among the positive qualities she mentioned, there were some developmental ones. 'You don't exactly eat up work' she said, 'I don't see you driving for results'. When I saw the listing above it made me remember this feedback and I thought 'Well, she wouldn't say that if she knew me now.'

But this chapter is not about expounding the virtues of being driven. It's about just the opposite. Sometimes we do need to drive our career, for sure, but there are also times when we need to slow right down.

A client sat in front of me, clearly exhausted. So tired that he was struggling to get his thoughts together to respond to my questions. He was fast on the way to burning out. That's why he was coming to see me. Struggling to do a job which was no longer fulfilling was something he had recognised he didn't want to go on doing, so he has begun the process of searching for a career which is more satisfying and which is likely to energise him instead of draining him of energy.

But reviewing your life in the way in which he is doing is something that, in itself, needs plenty of energy and when you're drained that's not the best time to do it. If your energy is low, it's all you can do to keep going with the daily routine, without searching for your future direction at the same time. We both recognised that he needs to take some time out to recharge his batteries before he can move on effectively. So he's gone away to take some space and relax a bit.

Sometimes it's hard, when we desperately want to make changes and move on in our lives, to take time out to stop, but often it's necessary to give us the focus we need.

I remembered reading in a book on change that we have to slow down to turn a corner. Sure, and the sharper the corner and the less familiar the territory, the slower we have to be on approach, if we don't want to come a cropper.

In the work which I do, I often see people making big changes in their lives – some major shifts towards something they'd never believed was possible. It's wonderful. Change is great but you have to make space for it. Sometimes when we keep stoically hurtling on we become blinkered and therefore not open to the possibilities around us, and this is especially the case when we're in a situation which we're not finding comfortable, because all our energy is focused on just keeping going.

Stopping to take stock isn't going to take the same form for everyone. For some people it might be a couple of hours, for some people a couple of weeks, for some it might even be a lot longer – career breaks lasting up to two years are no longer so unusual. You'll know what feels right for you, enough to provide the recharge that you need.

And if you don't take it, it can claim you! I hear so many times of people being forced to stop, even though it was never their intention. Sometimes clients tell me that they are unable to complete a project because of delays due to external factors; sometimes they have a bout of illness which forces them to stop. Often we are presented with a break, whether we'd planned it or not, and then we find it's just what we needed in order to get that reflection time – the ability to put everything in perspective.

Make space for change:

- Know where to go to recharge your batteries – whatever works for you – exercise, meditation, that special location, fishing, just 'away' somewhere.
- Give yourself time off. Even if you're job searching, allow yourself some time to yourself and to get a break from the routine.
- Don't be judgmental on yourself, and don't allow others to be judgmental – no 'shoulds' – do what feels right for you.

- Allow yourself to explore ideas about potential and creativity, however wacky they seem. This might include childhood ambitions or fantasy projects – don't censor anything.
- Allow your thoughts to come up to the surface. Take a look at the negative ones and then dismiss them.
- Track the positive and surprising thoughts. Keep a journal. Make notes but don't analyse them until your 'time out' is through.

SO, NOW WHAT?

I started this book with several questions which are posed to me in my role as career coach, and through the chapters I've given some guidance on how you may begin to answer those questions.

What I've aimed to do is to give you some clear direction about techniques and principles which underly career issues - tools to support you in your decision-making and knowledge of how the jobsearch scene actually operates, so that you are now armed with some facts and tangibles and can use these to build confidence in taking action in your search for a more fulfilling career.

I also aimed to encourage you to consider how to apply these general principles in the context of your own life. My hope is that, even though you might have a burning career issue right now, that you're able to see how applying some of these ideas could benefit your ability, not just to address your current career issue, but also to manage your career on an ongoing basis in a proactive way.

This is good career management. What I aim to do with clients is not just to help them to find a solution to the immediate and pressing issue with which they are grappling, but also to provide them with some skills and, more importantly, the right perspective to help them to feel more in control from now on and to take charge of their career for themselves.

However, we all need support from time to time, even if we're going it alone, and I've mentioned through the book some people who have inspired me. One man's inspiration is another man's irritation, though, so I'll spare you a list of Claire's gurus, but it can be useful to think about who inspires you and how, because you can get support from those sources as you progress. It may be a particular writer, a leader or a friend. Tapping into their thoughts and opinions can be a way of clarifying your own ideas and keeping you focused.

What I have done on the following pages is to provide a bibliography, so if you're interested you can begin to follow through for yourself and build your own support network to suit you. If you'd like more information, then take a look at my Web site www.adastra-cm.com

Life is not static and there are great opportunities out there which are yours for the taking. What they require from you is a willingness to explore what's there and a readiness to learn about yourself. Keep evaluating how you are developing and what your changing needs are; consider how these fit with what's happening in the external world; have conversations; take action; keep it moving.

So, over to you, take charge, begin to find that career satisfaction which you deserve, and enjoy!

BIBLIOGRAPHY

Books for Section 1 -

'I'm sure that I have more to offer to the experience of work than this - how do I begin to find out?'

Snap, crackle or stop by Barbara Quinn, Momentum, 2001

This book is for people who are thinking about career change, from the perspective of the 'snap' of not being able to take it one day longer in the current role or the slow painful crackle of creeping discontent. Using case studies for encouragement (there are hosts of people who do actually make the break), it looks at why we stay in a job far longer than we feel we should, and drives us to action through honestly evaluating our situation.

Unconditional Success by Nick Williams, Bantam, 2003

Somehow we get to adulthood with the belief that success is for the few. We also tend to hold negative associations about success. Nick dismantles these ideas, instead replacing them with a new success ethic based on 'creating a new match between who we are in essence and what we do in the world'.

The exercises and examples provide gentle challenge and the 'wisdom questions' which Nick poses are deceptively simple, but they very pow-

erfully get to the heart of understanding our experience of work and
success.

How to get a job you'll love by John Lees, McGraw Hill, 2003

There are plenty of books around on different aspects of managing your career. Based on the premise that we all invent creative solutions to everyday problems - 'taking children in opposite directions in one car; paying this week's bill with next week's money', John Lees adopts a right-brain approach in solving career issues. This has plenty of appeal, because if things aren't working for you in terms of achieving a satisfying career, then you probably need to take a different - more creative - approach.

What colour is your parachute? by Richard Bolles, Ten Speed Press, 2003

The classic book for career changers, 'What colour is your parachute?' is lively and visually appealing enough to comfortably find a place in someone's Christmas stocking, yet it provides a focused and direct tool for approaching career change.

Callings by Gregg Levoy, Three Rivers Press, 1998

Part of the challenge of mid-life review is getting clarity about what it is you feel led to do. Gregg Levoy encourages us to take a hard look at those messages about our direction – our calling – which we may have been ignoring, perhaps for decades.
This is not a quick fix and you won't find a one-size-fits-all solution. What this book provides is a kind of prism through which you see your life in a different way. It is at times humorous as well as being comforting and challenging and is essentially a practical guide for finding our way.

What Should I Do With My Life - the true story of people who answered the ultimate question by Po Bronson, Vintage, 2003

This book is, quite simply, a collection of chronicles about ordinary people who try to find their 'calling'. As the author says – 'when I say that these are ordinary people, I mean they're real, they're messy and complicated'. These are stories of people's gambles to follow their dreams.

This is inspiring not because they are all success stories - some stories are of failure - but because they are people who try to make some greater sense of their lives. It's a powerful book because it's simple and may help you to find a way to move your own story on.

Happy Mondays by Richard Reeves, Momentum, 2001

This book takes an uncompromising view that the bad press which work receives is outdated and irrelevant. Richard Reeves challenges many of the so-called problems of modern life - that high turnover reflects job insecurity, that increased hours at work are destroying family life, that community and spiritual life is less important, by claiming that people are finding a new fulfilment at work.

Books for Section 2 -
'I believe that there could be a couple of options for my future career – how do I decide what's best for me?

Brilliant future - work out what you want and plan how to get there by Chris Sangster, Prentice Hall, 2002

This is more a workbook than a text book and provides a focus for understanding your personal style, how you operate and how you can get the best out of your situation. Clear and focused with sound advice.

What Next? - The complete guide to taking control of your working life by Barbara Moses, Dorling Kindersley, 2003

As career guidance books go, this one is pretty all-encompassing. Barbara Moses covers all the usual career stuff such as writing a CV and preparing for interviews, but she also covers broader career issues such as overcoming career crises and dealing with difficult bosses. This is helpful as we all know that it's one thing to find a great role but another to experience ongoing satisfaction in the workplace.

Powerful beyond measure by Nick Williams, Bantam, 2003

We learn to see power as relational - we can only have power at the expense of others, and vice versa. We therefore attribute power with negative connotations and believe that it can only be achieved through becoming a different person, one we don't necessarily want to be - and usually if someone else will allow us to change.

Nick Williams shows us a different perspective which is based on finding the power within us rather than searching for something outside of us which doesn't feel comfortable. It's about being rather than doing and letting power emerge. He takes us through exercises which help to dispel the myths which we grew up with surrounding the concept of power and encourages us to see that we can all become powerful - it's just a case of finding it, knowing where to look.

The Luck Factor by Richard Wiseman, Century, 2003

This book is based on research into how life unfolds for people who consider themselves to be lucky and people who consider themselves to be unlucky. Following the outline of research, Wiseman then goes on to teach you how to turn your fortunes so that you can give your own luck a boost.

This is an extremely readable and practical book, packed with case studies, ways of assessing your own luckiness and a variety of exercises for creating a changed attitude. Try it!

Working Identity - unconventional strategies for reinventing your career by Herminia Ibarra, Harvard Business School Press, 2003

Ibarra turns conventional wisdom on its head. We are told that in order to make change we must know what we want to do. Ibarra challenges this to say that we only know what we want to do by acting and then evaluating and reviewing those actions to shape our knowledge.

With two key premises at the core of the book - 1. there are many possibilities for change, and 2. changing career means changing ourselves, Ibarra explores thirty-nine case studies to demonstrate how powerful and effective the change process can be.

Books for Section 3 -
'The job search scene has changed since I was last looking - how do I approach it and market myself effectively?

Managing Brand Me by Thomas Gad and Anette Rosencreutz, Momentum, 2002

'Brand Me' sounds a bit offputting, doesn't it? A bit Californian. Don't let that deter you from reading it, it's an excellent book. You, too, like David Beckham, Audrey Hepburn, Richard Branson and a whole host of other people can develop your own 'brand' to enable you to stand out from the crowd.

Yet another one from the Momentum series and they always hit the spot. Focused, practical and easy to work through without being patronising.

Brilliant CV - What Employers Want to See and How to Say It by Jim Bright and Joanne Earl, Prentice Hall, 2005

This is a lively and direct book which operates on the basis that readers may not know anything at all about CVs, so is useful for those who really don't have a clue. Through use of plenty of humour and oodles of examples, the authors get the message over effectively and painlessly. This is an easy-to-work-through book which is visually appealing as well as having sound content.

Interviews made easy by Mark Parkinson, Kogan Page, 1998

Building on the idea that an interview is a two-way process where the interviewee can, and should, take an active role, Mark Parkinson approaches the interview as a game, and in this small but concise volume, goes about explaining the rules.

In other words, this book demystifies the interview process. It starts off by providing a background to the job search process and covers the different routes to interview, through newspaper advertisements and agencies to networking, but the book comes into its own, perhaps not surprisingly, when it's dealing with the interview itself.

Powerful networking by John Lockett, Orion, 2000

An easy-to-read guide to developing networking skills, which assesses your particular networking style and encourages you to build on that, rather than adopt a style which doesn't feel comfortable.

My situation means that I have to stay put in this job for a while – how do I make the best of it?

The Tipping Point - how little things can make a big difference by Malcolm Gladwell, Abacus, 2000

What a great book! As readable and absorbing as any truly good novel, it explores the phenomenon whereby suddenly something becomes big, a force to be reckoned with. Malcolm Gladwell analyses a range of phenomena, from medical epidemics to shopping trends to social issues, getting at the heart of why this idea/trend/disease took off at that particular time – what were the elements which conspired to shift the way that it was previously experienced, and catapult it into another league.

The first 90 days – critical success strategies for new leaders at all levels by Michael Watkins, Harvard Business School Press, 2003

This one is apparently doing the rounds of friends who have recently started new jobs. As the title suggests, this book is aimed at those new to leadership roles, but it's worth a look for anyone making a new start.

Giant Steps - small changes to make a big difference by Anthony Robbins, Simon & Schuster, 2001

'Giant Steps' is a distillation of the key hints and tips of Robbins' earlier book and is an absolute gem. Open it randomly and you'll be hit between the eyes with a solution to something that's been eluding you for years. He is able to reframe absolutely any situation to see the positive aspects and the learning from it.

How to get what you want in the workplace: a practical guide for improving communication and getting results by John Gray, Vermilion, 2003

You might recognise John Gray as the guy who wrote the hugely successful 'Men are from Mars, women are from Venus' and here he applies his approach beyond intimate relationships and into the workplace.

This book is, at it says, practical and as you might expect from a book about communication, easy to read, explaining communication styles and misunderstanding in simple terms, with plenty of hints and tips for adopting different behaviours. Some of the gender-based examples are quite stereotypical, but if you accept this for what it is, a simple communication guide, I'd say it was worth reading and is exceptionally good value.

The big difference - life works when you choose it by Nicola Phillips, Momentum, 2001

As with the others in the Momentum series, this is essentially a practical manual for dealing with life in all its glory. Powerful and energising, a great guide.

Books for Section 5 -
'There's more to life than work - what about the bigger picture?'

Authentic Happiness by Martin Seligman, Nicolas Brealey, 2002

Seligman's wide-ranging book talks about the three pillars of positive psychology – positive emotion, positive traits and positive institutions. Clearly, the approach is that if we understand and embrace the first we can build the second, and through that the third will evolve. This idea is expressed through much New Age writing, but as far as I'm concerned, that's no reason not to give it a try.

The Living Workplace by Ann Coombs, Harper Business, 2001

The Living Workplace, subtitled Soul, Spirit and Success in the 21st Century, is a vision of tomorrow's workplace, a workplace which accommodates employees' demands for a lifestyle, every hour of every day, which is about quality of life and recognition of values, as opposed to the Toxic Workplace, defined as 'a place where people come to work so that they can make enough money to leave it'.

About The Author

Claire has a track record of success in providing career coaching and advice at all organisational levels and across all sectors. With a degree in psychology and a particular interest in personality and motivation, she has extensive experience of working with individuals to enhance self-awareness and working relationships.

Keen to quickly get to the heart of each individual's specific career issues, her approach is to enable people to evaluate, understand and maximise their personal resources and the opportunities around them, in order to gain greater fulfilment in their work and life experiences.

Claire is a member of the British Psychological Society, the Association of Business Psychologists and is currently the United Kingdom President for the Association of Career Professionals International.

www.adastra-cm.com

Printed in the United Kingdom by
Lightning Source UK Ltd., Milton Keynes
140524UK00002B/98/A